Microwave Cooking · Fruits & Vegetables

Litton Microwave Cooking Products, Minneapolis, Minnesota

from Litton

CERTIFIED FOR
MICROWAVE COOKING

LITTON
Microwave
Cooking
Center

CREDITS
Design & Production: Cy DeCosse Creative Department, Inc.
Authors: Barbara Methven, Sara Jean Thoms
Art Director: Nancy McDonough
Production Coordinators: Julia Slott, Christine Watkins
Photographers: Michael Jensen, Buck Holzemer, Ken Greer
Food Stylists: Maria Rolandelli, Suzanne Finley, Lucinda Kircher, Carol Grones
Home Economists: Peggy Lamb, Jill Crum, Carol Grones
Consumer Testers: Anne Antolak, Gail Bailey, Gloria Johnson, Judith Richard
Color Separations: Weston Engraving Co., Inc.
Printing: Moebius Printing Co.

This is no ordinary recipe book. It's like a cooking school in your home, ready to answer questions on the spot. Step-by-step photographs show you how to prepare food for microwaving, what to do during cooking, how to tell when the food is done. A new photo technique shows you how foods look during microwaving.

The foods selected for this book are basic in several ways. All microwave well and demonstrate the advantages of microwaving. They are popular foods you prepare frequently, so the book will be useful in day-to-day cooking. Each food illustrates a principle or technique of microwaving which you can apply to similar recipes you find in magazines or other cookbooks.

This book was designed to obtain good results in all brands of ovens. Techniques may vary from the cookbook developed for your oven. If rotating foods is unnecessary in your oven, that technique may be eliminated. All foods are cooked at either High or 50% power (Medium). The Defrost setting on earlier ovens and Simmer setting on current ovens may be used when Medium is called for. This simplifies the choice of settings while you become familiar with the reasons why different foods require different power levels.

Microwaving is easy as well as fast. The skills you develop with this book will help you make full and confident use of your microwave oven.

The Litton Microwave
Cooking Center

Contents

What You Need to Know Before You Start

The exceptional quality of microwaved vegetables and fruits is an outstanding benefit of the microwave oven. Rapid cooking in a minimum of water is the surest way to retain nutrients. In addition, microwaving preserves the taste, texture and color of fresh produce. To enjoy vegetables and fruits at the peak of flavor, you should know how to buy and store them as well as how to microwave them.

Select Quality Produce

Most cooks instinctively avoid the obvious signs of poor quality. They check fruits and vegetables for withering or decay. However, they may not know the tests of high quality or the signs which indicate that fresh looking produce is under or overmature, and will have inferior flavor. In each section of this book you will find descriptions and color photographs that will help you select fruits and vegetables at their best.

Store Produce Properly

Some fruits and vegetables need time to ripen, soften or develop flavor; others have excellent keeping quality. Most begin to lose moisture as soon as they are picked, and will taste best when used as soon as possible.

Proper temperature and humidity are the keys to storage. Each fruit and vegetable has a temperature and humidity which keep it best. They are not all the same. The average home cannot provide optimum storage conditions for every type of produce; this book suggests the best storage available under normal home conditions.

The crisper is a drawer, bin or tray, found in most refrigerators, which is sealed off from the main compartment by a lid. The air in the crisper is warmer and more humid than the air in the rest of the refrigerator. This provides ideal storage for items which need to be kept cool and humid. Produce should not be sprinkled with water or washed before storage because that encourages decay.

The refrigerator shelves are exposed to circulating cold air. Humidity is fairly low, especially in a frost-free refrigerator. When produce should be kept cold and dry, store it on an open shelf. Items which require cold temperatures but higher humidity can be placed in plastic bags or an airtight container and stored in the coldest area.

Room temperature storage is best for fruits which need to ripen or soften, and for vegetables which are sensitive to cold and humidity. Fruits can be placed on the kitchen counter or in a ripening bowl. A mesh bag, hung in a chilly closet, is excellent for vegetables which need cool, dry, well-ventilated and dark storage.

Microwave Until Tender-Crisp

The recipes and time charts in this book are for vegetables and fruits which are tender, and have lost their raw taste, but are not mushy. They soften further on standing. If you prefer very soft vegetables or fruits, add more water and microwave longer.

3

Food Characteristics

Quality is the most important factor in microwaving fruits and vegetables. Fresh, tender produce needs only a minimum of water and a short microwaving time to become tender-crisp.

Size. Small pieces cook faster and more evenly than large ones, because energy can penetrate to the center from all sides. Allow ample standing time when cooking large, whole vegetables and fruits.

Quantity. Small amounts cook faster than large ones. Times in this book are for 1 to 4 units, such as ears of corn; 4 servings or 2 cups of pieces, such as sliced carrots; or an average package, such as a 1 to 1½-lb. bunch of broccoli.

Starting Temperature. Chilled vegetables and fruits take longer to cook than those at room temperature. Microwaving times in this book are for produce stored as recommended.

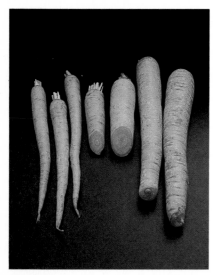

Quality. Moisture content and maturity directly affect cooking times. Fresh vegetables contain more natural moisture and microwave faster, with less water, than vegetables picked late in the season.

Density. Vegetables like broccoli and asparagus, which have tender ends and tougher stalks, should be arranged with stalks to the outside of the dish. Rotate dish after half the time.

Firm Skins. Prick or cut the skins of whole vegetables like potatoes or winter squash so steam can escape.

Microwaving Techniques

Use the same microwaving techniques for fruits and vegetables as you do for other foods. Of these, standing time is most important and most often neglected. Remember that if food is not done to your taste after standing, you can always microwave it longer.

Cover most vegetables with a casserole lid or vented plastic wrap to hold in moisture and speed microwaving.

Arrange whole or halved vegetables in a ring in oven or dish, leaving space between them, if possible. Rearrange vegetables or rotate dish after half the microwaving time.

Stir small vegetables and pieces from outside to center of dish after half the cooking time to equalize heat.

Turn over whole vegetables after half the cooking time. When cooking more than one, rearrange so items near center of oven are to the outside.

Let stand as directed in charts. Large or dense vegetables and fruits require more standing time so the center can tenderize without overcooking the exterior.

Salt vegetables after cooking, or dissolve it thoroughly in water before adding vegetables, to avoid dry or discolored spots.

Cutting Vegetables & Fruits for Microwaving

Many vegetables and fruits microwave faster and more evenly when they are cut into pieces. The microwaving charts give directions for the familiar slices, cubes, lengths or chunks, but you may cut vegetables in a variety of ways and achieve a similar piece size with a different appearance.

Roll cut. Hold carrot, parsnip or other long vegetable flat on cutting board. Make a diagonal slice straight down. Roll vegetable ¼ turn and slice again. Microwave for the same time as 2-in. cuts.

Wedge cut. Hold carrot or other long vegetable butt end down, at a 45° angle. Cut and turn as in sharpening a pencil, making ¼-in. slices or small chunks. Microwave for the same time as ¼-in. slices.

Flowers. Cut 5 or 6 small lengthwise notches in carrot. Slice vegetable. This cut is attractive in soups and combos.

Score. Hold tines of fork against zucchini. Pull fork the length of squash, making grooves in skin. Slice ¼ inch thick.

Bias Cut. Place long vegetable flat on board. Make diagonal cut straight down. Cut celery, carrots or zucchini diagonally into ½-in. thick slices and green beans or asparagus in lengths.

Crinkle cut. Special tool for this cut is found in housewares section of markets, hardware or department stores. Place firm vegetable, like potato or carrot on board. Cut straight down into crosswise or bias slices or lengthwise strips.

Half moon cut. Halve potatoes, turnips, carrots or zucchini lengthwise. Place flat side down on board. Slice.

Quarter moon cut. Quarter large, round vegetables like turnips, potatoes or rutabagas. Slice across each quarter into ⅛-in. thick pieces.

Julienne. Divide vegetables like carrots, parsnips, zucchini or potatoes into 2 to 3-in. lengths. Cut each piece lengthwise into ¼-in. thick slices. Slice again into ¼-in. thick strips.

How to Section Citrus Fruit

Slice off ends of fruit. Using a sawing motion, peel in spiral. Remove membrane, leaving as much fruit as possible.

Hold fruit over bowl to catch juice. Cut to center between fruit segment and dividing membrane with sharp knife.

Twist knife to free section from membrane on other side. Repeat until all fruit is removed; squeeze juice from membranes.

Seasonal Availability Charts

These charts show general availability as well as the peak season for fruits and vegetables featured in this book. The peak season for home-grown produce varies with the locality. No peak season is indicated for foods which do not exhibit a significant increase in availability, such as bananas and potatoes, which are plentiful year-round, or specialty items like Jerusalem artichokes, which are in limited supply.

■ Peak Availability
▨ General Availability
□ Not Available

Fruit Availability Chart

Fruits	Jan.	Feb.	Mar.	Apr.	May	June	July	Aug.	Sept.	Oct.	Nov.	Dec.
Apples	Peak	Peak	Peak	Gen.	Gen.	Gen.	Gen.	Gen.	Peak	Peak	Peak	Peak
Apricots						Peak	Peak					
Bananas,	Gen.	Gen.	Gen.	Gen.	Gen.	Gen.	Gen.	Gen.	Gen.	Gen.	Gen.	Gen.
Plantains	Gen.	Gen.	Gen.	Gen.	Gen.	Peak	Peak	Peak	Peak	Peak	Gen.	Gen.
Berries: Blackberries						Peak	Peak	Gen.				
Blueberries						Peak	Peak	Gen.				
Cranberries									Gen.	Peak	Peak	Gen.
Raspberries						Peak	Peak	Gen.	Gen.			
Strawberries				Gen.	Peak	Peak	Gen.					
Cherries						Peak	Gen.					
Citrus Fruit: Grapefruit	Peak	Peak	Peak	Peak	Peak	Gen.	Gen.	Gen.	Gen.	Gen.	Gen.	Gen.
Lemons	Gen.	Gen.	Gen.	Gen.	Gen.	Gen.	Gen.	Gen.	Gen.	Gen.	Gen.	Gen.
Limes	Gen.	Gen.	Gen.	Gen.	Gen.	Peak	Peak	Peak	Gen.	Gen.	Gen.	Gen.
Navel Oranges	Peak	Peak	Peak	Peak	Peak	Gen.					Peak	Peak
Valencia Oranges	Gen.	Gen.	Gen.	Peak	Peak	Peak	Gen.	Gen.	Gen.	Gen.	Gen.	Gen.
Dates, Figs, Raisins	Gen.	Gen.	Gen.	Gen.	Gen.	Gen.	Gen.	Gen.	Gen.	Gen.	Gen.	Gen.
Grapes	Gen.	Gen.	Gen.	Gen.	Gen.	Gen.	Gen.	Peak	Peak	Peak	Gen.	Gen.
Nectarines						Gen.	Peak	Peak	Gen.			
Peaches					Gen.	Peak	Peak	Peak	Gen.			
Pears	Gen.	Gen.	Gen.	Gen.	Gen.	Gen.	Gen.	Peak	Peak	Peak	Gen.	Gen.
Pineapple	Gen.	Gen.	Peak	Peak	Peak	Peak	Gen.	Gen.	Gen.	Gen.	Gen.	Gen.
Plums						Peak	Peak	Peak	Peak	Gen.		
Prunes								Gen.	Peak	Peak	Gen.	
Rhubarb			Peak	Peak	Peak	Gen.						

Vegetable Availability Chart

Vegetables	Jan.	Feb.	Mar.	Apr.	May	June	July	Aug.	Sept.	Oct.	Nov.	Dec.
Artichokes			X	X	X							
Asparagus			X	X	X	X						
Beans: Green, Wax					X	X	X	X				
Limas, Dried Legumes												
Beets						X	X	X	X			
Broccoli	X	X	X	X						X	X	X
Brussels Sprouts	X	X	X	X						X	X	X
Cabbage: Bok Choy	X	X	X	X							X	X
Chinese	X	X		X						X	X	X
Green, Red	X	X										X
Savoy												
Carrots												
Cauliflower	X								X	X	X	
Celery												
Corn					X	X	X	X				
Eggplant							X	X				
Greens: Lettuce												
Other Greens	X	X	X									
Jerusalem Artichokes												
Jicama												
Kohlrabi							X	X				
Leeks			X									
Mushrooms	X											X
Okra						X	X	X				
Onions												
Peas: Garden or English												X
Snow or China					X	X	X	X				
Black-eyed												
Dried Peas												
Peppers: Sweet						X	X	X				
Potatoes												
Rutabagas, Parsnips, Turnips	X	X	X							X	X	X
Squash: Summer						X	X	X				
Winter									X	X	X	
Sweet Potatoes, Yams	X	X	X							X	X	X
Tomatoes					X	X	X	X				

Vegetables

Blanching & Freezing Vegetables

The microwave oven is an ideal way to blanch small batches of fresh vegetables for the freezer. If you are a home gardener, harvest young, tender vegetables as they reach the peak of flavor, rather than trying to preserve the whole crop at one time.

For best results, do not increase the quantities given in the chart. If you wish to blanch several batches, microwave the first while you clean and trim the second. Your kitchen will stay cool, and the small batches will be more uniform and easier to handle than a steamy kettleful blanched conventionally.

Blanching inactivates enzymes to preserve the vitamin content of vegetables stored in the freezer. Cook green vegetables only until they change color.

Others should be pliable but not tender. A single batch may be packed in small freezer boxes or heat sealable pouches to make a block of vegetables which will be easy to defrost and microwave. If you wish to pack vegetables in large bags or boxes, use the loose-pack method so you can remove the amount needed and return the rest to the freezer.

How to Blanch Fresh Vegetables

Clean vegetables thoroughly. Cut vegetables into small pieces, if possible. Slices, 1-in. lengths or flowerets microwave and freeze easily.

Place pieces in casserole with water; cover. Microwave, following times in chart, until vegetables are vibrant green or pliable but crisp. Drain.

Plunge vegetables immediately into ice water to cool completely. This prevents further cooking. Drain thoroughly.

Pack small amounts tightly into freezer bags, boxes or pouches, leaving ½-in. airspace at top of package. Seal.

Loose-pack for large containers by spreading pieces on baking sheet. Freeze, then pack in bags or boxes and seal.

Label plainly with name of vegetable and date. Frozen blanched vegetables will keep for 9 to 12 months at 0° F.

Blanching Fresh Vegetables Chart

Type	Amount	Microwave Time at High	Procedure
Beans			
Green, Wax	½ lb. (2 cups)	5-6 min.	1½-in. pieces. 3-qt. covered casserole with 1 cup water. Stir twice.
Lima	¾ lb. (2 cups)	3½-5 min.	3-qt. covered casserole with 1 cup water. Stir once.
Broccoli			
Pieces	4 cups	4-5½ min.	3-qt. covered casserole with 1 cup water. Stir twice.
Brussels Sprouts			
Whole	2-2½ cups	4-5 min.	2-qt. covered casserole with 1 cup water. Stir once.
Carrots			
Slices, ⅛-in.	2 cups	4½-6 min.	3-qt. covered casserole with 1 cup water. Stir once.
Cauliflower			
Flowerets	2 cups	4-4½ min.	3-qt. covered casserole with 1 cup water. Stir once.
Greens			
Spinach, leaves	1-1¼ lb.	4-5 min.	3-qt. covered casserole with 1 cup water. Stir twice.
Swiss chard, leaves	1 lb.	3½-4 min.	3-qt. covered casserole with 1 cup water. Stir twice.
Turnip, leaves	1 lb.	4½-6½ min.	3-qt. covered casserole with 1 cup water. Stir twice.
Okra			
Whole or Pieces, ½-in.	¾ lb.	4½-5½ min.	3-qt. covered casserole with 1 cup water. Stir twice.
Peas			
Whole	2 cups	4-5 min.	3-qt. covered casserole with 1 cup water. Stir once.
Squash			
Yellow, Zucchini, slices, ¼-in.	2 cups	3½-4 min.	3-qt. covered casserole with 1 cup water. Stir once.

Frozen & Canned Vegetables

Freezing and canning make your favorite vegetables available at any season of the year. Some vegetables, like baby peas, are rarely found in fresh form because most of the crop is frozen or canned. Others, like whole kernel corn, are usually prepared frozen or canned because of their convenience and quality.

In each of the vegetable charts you will find directions for microwaving frozen and canned varieties. Some popular vegetables are available in several forms. Step by step techniques for loose-pack or boxed frozen vegetables, frozen pouches and canned vegetables are demonstrated here. Follow directions in the charts for casserole size, liquid, cooking and standing times.

How to Microwave Canned Vegetables

Reserve 1 or 2 tablespoons liquid from can of vegetables as directed on chart.

Drain remaining liquid. Pour vegetables with reserved liquid into casserole. Cover.

Microwave at High for time recommended on chart, stirring after half the time.

How to Microwave Frozen Vegetables

Place vegetables in casserole with water recommended in chart. If vegetables are frozen in a block, turn icy side up. Cover.

Microwave at High for half the cooking time. Stir to break apart pieces and redistribute heat.

Cover. Microwave remaining time. Let stand, covered, for the time indicated in the chart.

How to Microwave Frozen Vegetable Pouches

Flex pouch to break apart vegetables, if possible. With a knife, cut a large "X" in one side of pouch.

Place pouch, cut side down, in 1-qt. casserole. Microwave at High for the time recommended in the chart for that vegetable.

Lift corners on far side of pouch, so your hands are protected from steam as vegetable is released into dish. Stir, cover and let stand as directed in chart.

Artichokes

An artichoke is the edible flower of a thistle. Medium or large artichokes may be eaten leaf-by-leaf, hot or cold, dipped in melted butter or a sauce. Stuff large artichokes with chicken, seafood or egg salad.

Artichoke "hearts", sold frozen or canned, are immature globes without chokes and are completely edible. Serve them pickled or in salads, stews or casseroles. The prickly choke of a mature globe must be

scraped away as the artichoke is eaten or before it is stuffed. Below the choke is the succulent bottom. Artichoke bottoms can be used to hold vegetables, creamed fillings, or poached eggs.

How to Select Artichokes

Choose firm, plump globes, heavy for their size, with tightly closed leaves. In spring, artichokes should be bright green. During the winter months, leaves may be bronzed by frost but quality is not impaired. Avoid artichokes with loose, spreading leaves; they are over-mature and will be tough.

How to Store Artichokes

Store artichokes in a perforated plastic bag in the refrigerator. Use within a few days. Cooked artichokes keep well for several days when tightly covered in the refrigerator.

How to Prepare & Microwave Artichokes

Trim artichokes 1 in. from top and close to base so it will stand. Snap off small lower leaves and snip tips of outer leaves. Rinse; shake off water.

Brush with lemon juice to prevent discoloration. Wrap in plastic wrap, or place in 8 × 8-in. baking dish with ¼ cup water; cover with plastic wrap.

Microwave until lower leaves can be pulled off, and base pierces easily. Rotate and rearrange after half the time. See chart for cooking times.

Artichoke Chart

Type	Amount	Microwave Time at High	Procedure
Fresh Artichokes Whole	1 2 3 4	4-5 min. 5½-8½ min. 8½-11½ min. 9½-14½ min.	Follow photo directions above. Let stand 3 to 5 minutes.
Frozen Artichokes Artichoke Hearts	9 oz. pkg.	5-6 min.	1-qt. covered casserole with 2 tablespoons water. Stir after first 2 minutes. Let stand 2 minutes.

◄ Stuffed Artichokes

4 medium artichokes
¼ cup lemon juice
¼ cup water
¼ cup chopped green onion
¼ cup chopped celery
1 clove garlic, pressed or
    minced
1 tablespoon butter or
    margarine

1 pkg. (12 oz.) frozen spinach
    soufflé, defrosted*
½ cup fine dry bread crumbs
1½ teaspoons parsley flakes
    Dash pepper
½ cup shredded Cheddar
    cheese

Serves 4

Trim artichokes 1 inch from top and close to base. Cut off sharp tips of outer leaves; brush with lemon juice. In 8 × 8-in. baking dish place artichokes and water. Cover tightly with plastic wrap. Microwave at High 6 minutes, or until just tender, rotating dish ½ turn after half the cooking time. Set aside.

In small dish microwave green onion, celery, garlic and butter at High 2 to 3 minutes, or until tender, stirring after half the cooking time. Stir in soufflé, bread crumbs, parsley and pepper. Open the center of each artichoke to form a well. Remove some of the center leaves and scrape out choke; stuff artichokes with spinach. Rearrange in 8 × 8-in. baking dish. Cover with plastic wrap.

Microwave at High 6 minutes, or until filling is hot, base is fork tender and leaves can be removed with slight tug, rotating dish ½ turn after half the cooking time. Sprinkle each artichoke with one-fourth of cheese. Re-cover. Microwave at High 1 to 2 minutes, or until cheese melts, rotating dish ½ turn after half the time.

*To defrost: Remove from foil package and place in small bowl. Microwave at 50% (Medium) 4 to 5 minutes, or until softened, breaking up with fork after half the cooking time.

Hot Artichoke Dip

1 pkg. (8 oz.) cream cheese
1 jar (6 oz.) marinated
    artichoke hearts, chopped
    and 1 tablespoon
    marinade reserved
⅓ cup dairy sour cream

2 tablespoons chopped green
    onion
1 tablespoon chopped
    pimiento
⅛ teaspoon red pepper sauce

Makes about 2 cups

In 1-qt. serving dish soften cream cheese at High 30 to 60 seconds, stirring after half the time, then every 15 seconds. Mix in remaining ingredients.

Reduce power to 50% (Medium). Microwave 3 to 6 minutes, or until mixture is hot, stirring after 2 minutes and then every minute.

Artichokes Vinaigrette ▶

2 pkgs. (9 oz. each) frozen
    artichoke hearts
2 tablespoons water

Marinade:
⅔ cup vegetable or olive oil
¼ cup white wine
¼ cup white vinegar
2 tablespoons chopped onion
1 tablespoon lemon juice
2 cloves garlic, pressed or
    minced

½ teaspoon parsley flakes
½ teaspoon chervil
½ teaspoon marjoram
½ teaspoon basil leaves
½ teaspoon salt
¼ teaspoon sugar
⅛ teaspoon tarragon
6 peppercorns
1 bay leaf

Serves 6 to 8

In 1½-qt. casserole place artichoke hearts and water. Cover.
Microwave at High 8 to 9 minutes, or until tender, stirring to break
up after half the cooking time.

Meanwhile combine marinade ingredients in small bowl or 2-cup
measure. Microwave at High 1 minute to blend flavors. Drain
artichokes; pour marinade over. Re-cover. Refrigerate at least 4
hours, stirring occasionally.

Stewed Artichokes

1 cup water, divided
½ teaspoon instant chicken
    bouillon granules
2 large potatoes, peeled and
    cut into ½-in. cubes
2 medium carrots, thinly sliced
1 large onion, chopped
2 tablespoons olive oil

½ teaspoon salt
⅛ teaspoon pepper
¼ teaspoon basil leaves
1 bay leaf
2 artichokes, rinsed and
    drained
2 tablespoons lemon juice

Serves 2 to 4

In 1-cup measure combine ¼ cup hot tap water and bouillon. Stir
to dissolve. In 3-qt. casserole combine dissolved bouillon,
potatoes, carrots, onion, oil, salt, pepper, basil and bay leaf. Cover.
Microwave at High 10 minutes, or until vegetables are tender-crisp,
stirring 2 or 3 times during cooking.

Trim artichokes 1 inch from top and close to base. Cut off sharp
tips of outer leaves; brush with lemon juice.

Stir remaining water into vegetable mixture. Add artichokes, cover
with plastic wrap. Microwave at High 14 to 16 minutes, or until
lower leaves of artichoke can be pulled off with a slight tug, stirring
vegetables, rearranging and basting artichokes 2 or 3 times during
cooking. Remove artichokes and bay leaf. Set aside. Purée
vegetable mixture. Serve artichokes with puréed vegetable mixture
as dip.

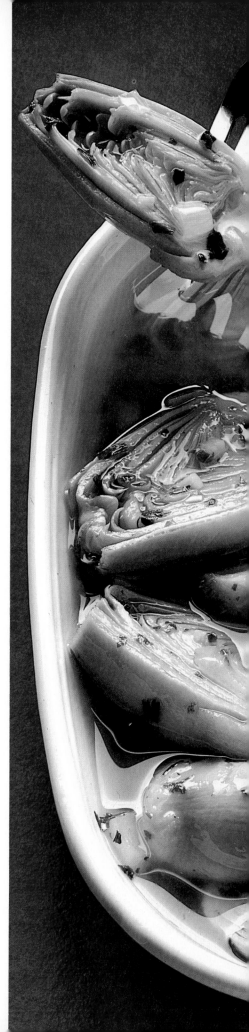

Asparagus

The first asparagus appears in early spring and a brief second crop is available in late summer, but the peak season is March through June. Most asparagus sold in the United States is green; a few markets may have hilled asparagus which is grown underground to keep it white. Asparagus of any size may be tender, but it is best to buy spears of uniform size so they will microwave evenly.

How to Select Asparagus

Look for tightly closed buds and firm, round stalks which are moist at the cut end. Both thick and thin spears are tender.

Avoid open, seedy tips and angular, ridged stalks which may be fibrous.

How to Store Asparagus

Asparagus should be kept cold and humid from the time it is picked. Wrap it in plastic, refrigerate, and use as soon as possible. If kept more than 3 days, its moisture will evaporate. Do not wash asparagus until ready to cook.

How to Prepare & Microwave Asparagus

Hold stalk firmly near butt. Gently bend spear until tough end snaps off. Cut away scales with sharp knife. Wash spears in cold water.

Measure ¼ cup water into 12 × 8-in. dish. Stir in ¼ teaspoon salt, sugar or honey.

Place 1 lb. spears in dish with buds toward center. Cover with plastic wrap.

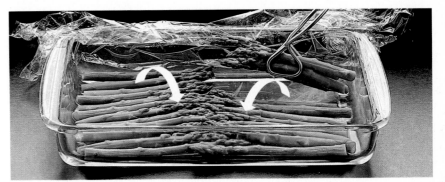

Microwave for half the time. Rearrange spears from outside to middle of dish, keeping buds in center. Cover. Microwave remaining time until tender-crisp. See chart for cooking times.

Asparagus Chart

Type	Amount	Microwave Time at High	Procedure
Fresh Asparagus			
Spears	1 lb.	6½-9½ min.	Follow photo directions above.
Cuts	1 lb.	5-7 min.	2-qt. covered casserole with ¼ cup water and ¼ teaspoon salt. Let stand 3 minutes.
Frozen Asparagus			
Spears	8-10 oz. pkg.	4½-5½ min.	1-qt. covered casserole with 2 tablespoons water. Rearrange once. Let stand 3 minutes.
Cuts	10 oz. pkg. (2 cups)	5-7 min.	1-qt. covered casserole with 2 tablespoons water. Stir once. Let stand 3 minutes.
In butter sauce	10 oz. pkg.	4-6½ min.	Flex pouch. Cut large X in one side. Place cut side down in 1-qt. casserole or serving dish. Stir before serving.
Canned Asparagus			
Spears, Cuts	15 oz.	2-4 min.	Drain all but 1 tablespoon liquid. 1-qt. covered casserole. Stir once.

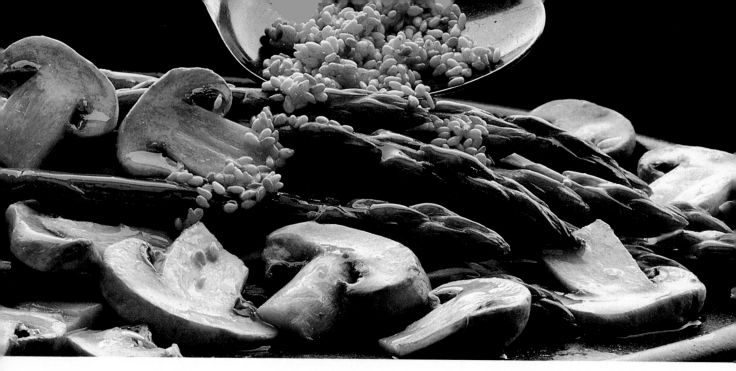

Asparagus, Mushrooms ▲ & Lemon Butter

1 lb. fresh asparagus spears
3 tablespoons butter or
   margarine, divided
2 teaspoons sesame seed
4 oz. fresh mushrooms, sliced
1 tablespoon lemon juice
½ teaspoon grated lemon peel

Serves 6 to 8

Prepare asparagus as directed, page 21.

Place 1 tablespoon butter in custard cup. Microwave at High 30 to 60 seconds, or until melted. Stir in sesame seeds. Microwave at High 3 to 5 minutes, or until brown, stirring once. Set aside.

Sprinkle mushrooms over asparagus; cover. Microwave at High 1 minute. Set aside. Melt remaining butter in small dish at High 30 to 60 seconds. Stir in lemon juice and peel.

Drain vegetables. Remove to serving platter. Drizzle lemon butter over top; sprinkle with sesame seed.

Variation:
Substitute 2 pkgs. (8 oz. each) frozen spears for fresh. To prepare, reduce water to 2 tablespoons and omit salt.

Asparagus Puff

1 lb. fresh asparagus, cut
   into 1-in. pieces or 1
   pkg. (10 oz.) frozen
   chopped asparagus
¼ cup chopped green onion
2 tablespoons butter or
   margarine

2 tablespoons all-purpose
   flour
½ teaspoon salt
⅛ teaspoon pepper
1½ cups dairy sour cream
3 eggs, separated
½ teaspoon cream of tartar

Serves 6

Prepare asparagus as directed, page 21. Drain; set aside. In 2-qt. casserole microwave onion and butter at High 1 to 2 minutes, or until tender. Stir in flour, salt and pepper. Add sour cream and slightly beaten egg yolks. In medium bowl beat egg whites and cream of tartar until stiff but not dry. Fold whites into yolk mixture.

Arrange half of asparagus in bottom of ring mold. Top with half of egg mixture. Repeat layers. Reduce power to 50% (Medium). Microwave 8 to 15 minutes, or until mixture appears set, rotating dish ¼ turn every 3 to 4 minutes. Invert onto serving plate to serve.

Asparagus Soup

1 lb. fresh asparagus, cut
   into 1-in. pieces, or 1
   pkg. (10 oz.) frozen
   chopped asparagus
½ cup chopped celery
¼ cup chopped onion
1 tablespoon butter or
   margarine

2 cups milk
1 can (10¾ oz.) cream of
   celery soup
½ teaspoon instant chicken
   bouillon granules
⅛ teaspoon salt
   Dash pepper
½ teaspoon chervil

Serves 4

Prepare asparagus as directed, page 21. Drain; set aside. In 2-qt. casserole combine celery, onion and butter; cover. Microwave at High 2 to 4 minutes, or until tender. Stir in remaining ingredients; cover. Microwave at High 5 to 6 minutes, or until heated; stir twice.

Cheesy Asparagus ▶

2 lbs. fresh asparagus, cut
    into 1 to 1½-in. pieces
¼ cup water
3 tablespoons butter or
    margarine, divided
¼ cup fine dry bread crumbs
¼ cup cashews
2 tablespoons all-purpose flour
¼ teaspoon salt
¼ teaspoon dry mustard
⅛ teaspoon pepper
1 cup milk
1 cup shredded Cheddar cheese

Serves 6 to 8

Variation:
Substitute 2 pkgs. (8 oz. each)
frozen cut asparagus spears
for fresh. Reduce water to 2
tablespoons.

How to Microwave Cheesy Asparagus

Combine asparagus and water in 1½-qt. casserole; cover. Microwave at High 8 to 12 minutes, or until tender, stirring once. Drain; set aside.

Melt 1 tablespoon butter in small bowl at High 30 to 60 seconds. Mix in bread crumbs and cashews. Set aside.

Melt remaining butter in 1-qt. measure at High 30 to 60 seconds. Stir in flour and seasonings. Blend in milk.

Microwave at High 3 to 5 minutes, or until thickened and bubbly, stirring after 2 minutes and then every minute.

Remove half of asparagus from casserole. Spread remaining asparagus evenly in dish; pour on half of sauce. Sprinkle half of cheese over sauce.

Repeat layers. Top with crumb mixture. Microwave at High 1 to 2 minutes, or until hot and bubbly, rotating dish ½ turn after half the time.

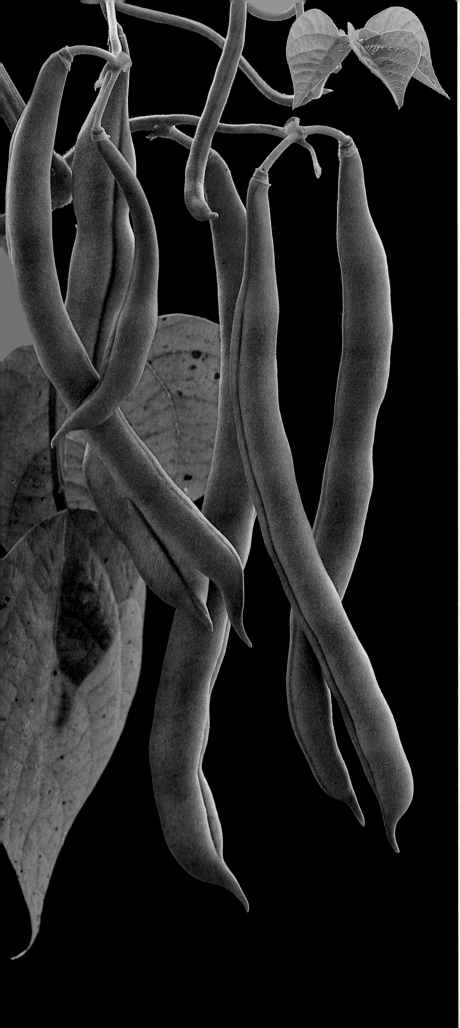

Beans: Green & Wax

Green and wax beans are available year-round, with the greatest supply from May through August. They are edible pods which are harvested before the seeds mature.

The size, shape and color of beans depends on their variety. Some types have a string which should be removed before cooking. For best flavor, use as soon as possible.

How to Select Green & Wax Beans

Choose firm, crisp beans which snap when bent and are free from scars. They should have small seeds and bright color for their variety.

Avoid flabby, thick, fibrous or very bumpy beans with well-developed seeds.

How to Store Beans

Place unwashed beans in a plastic bag or covered container to retain moisture. Refrigerate in the crisper and use within 2 days.

How to Prepare & Microwave Green & Wax Beans

Wash ½ lb. beans and remove stem and tip ends. Snap or cut into 1½ to 2-in. lengths.

Combine 2 cups bean pieces with ½ cup water in 1½-qt. casserole. Cover.

Microwave at High until tender-crisp, stirring once. See chart for cooking times.

Bean Chart

Type	Amount	Microwave Time at High	Procedure
Fresh Beans			
Green & Wax, cut	½ lb.	6-10 min.	Follow photo directions above. Let stand, covered, 2 to 3 minutes.
Frozen Beans			
Green & Wax, whole	9 oz. pkg. (2 cups)	6-7 min.	1-qt. covered casserole with 2 tablespoons water. Stir once. Let stand 3 minutes.
Green & Wax, cut	9 oz. pkg. (2 cups)	4-7 min.	1-qt. covered casserole with 2 tablespoons water. Stir once. Let stand 3 minutes.
French-style	9 oz. pkg.	5-7 min.	1-qt. covered casserole with 2 tablespoons water. Stir once. Let stand 3 minutes.
Italian-cut	9 oz. pkg.	6-8 min.	1-qt. covered casserole with 2 tablespoons water. Stir once. Let stand 3 minutes.
In butter sauce	9 oz. pkg.	4-6 min.	Flex pouch. Cut large X in one side. Place cut side down in 1-qt. casserole or serving dish. Stir before serving.
Canned Beans			
Green & Wax, whole, French-style, Italian-cut	16 oz.	2-4 min.	Drain all but 2 tablespoons liquid. 1-qt. covered casserole. Stir once.
Green & Wax, cut	15½ oz.	2-4 min.	Drain all but 2 tablespoons liquid. 1-qt. covered casserole. Stir once.

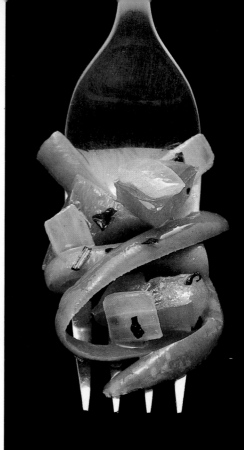

Sweet & Sour Beans ▲

1 lb. fresh green beans, cut
   into 1-in. pieces
⅓ cup water
2 tablespoons brown sugar
2 teaspoons cornstarch
3 tablespoons lemon juice
1 tablespoon butter or
   margarine

Topping:
¼ cup dry bread crumbs
¼ cup slivered almonds
1 tablespoon butter or
   margarine, softened
Dash nutmeg

Serves 6

In 1½ to 2-qt. casserole combine beans and water; cover. Microwave at High 9 to 11 minutes, or until tender-crisp, stirring after half the cooking time. Let stand 5 minutes. Drain, reserving ¼ cup liquid. Set beans aside.

In small bowl or 2-cup measure, combine brown sugar and cornstarch. Add lemon juice and reserved bean liquid. Microwave at High 1½ to 2 minutes, or until thickened, stirring after half the cooking time. Stir in butter.

Add thickened sauce mixture to beans. Combine topping ingredients. Sprinkle over beans. Microwave, uncovered, at High 1 to 1½ minutes.

Variations:

Substitute 2 pkgs. (9 oz. each) frozen cut green beans for fresh.

Substitute 2 cans (15½ oz. each) cut green beans for fresh. Drain, reserving ¼ cup bean liquid. Microwave beans and reserved liquid at High 3 to 4 minutes, or until thoroughly heated. Drain, reserving ¼ cup liquid. Continue as directed above.

Herbed Green Beans ▲

1 pkg. (9 oz.) frozen French
   style green beans
⅓ cup chopped green pepper
¼ cup chopped onion
1 tablespoon olive oil
1 tomato, peeled and chopped
½ teaspoon salt
¼ teaspoon sugar
¼ teaspoon basil leaves
⅛ teaspoon crushed rosemary
   Dash black pepper

Serves 4

Prepare beans as directed, page 25. Set aside.

In small bowl or 1-qt. casserole, combine green pepper, onion and oil. Microwave at High 1 to 2 minutes, or until tender.

Drain beans. Add green pepper mixture and remaining ingredients; cover. Microwave at High 1 to 2 minutes, or until heated.

Green Bean Casserole ▶

1 lb. fresh green beans, cut into 1 to 1½-in. pieces
⅓ cup water
1 can (10½ oz.) cream of mushroom soup
1 can (8 oz.) sliced water chestnuts, drained
¼ cup milk
1 can (4 oz.) mushroom stems and pieces, drained
1 can (3 oz.) French fried onion rings, divided
1 tablespoon soy sauce
¼ teaspoon salt
Dash pepper
1 teaspoon vinegar

Serves 6 to 8

Place beans and water in 2-qt. casserole; cover. Microwave at High 9 to 11 minutes, or until beans are tender, stirring after half the cooking time. Let stand 1 to 2 minutes. Drain.

Stir in soup, water chestnuts, milk, mushrooms, half the onion rings, soy sauce, salt, pepper and vinegar; cover. Microwave at High 3 to 5 minutes, or until thoroughly heated, stirring after half the cooking time. Stir. Sprinkle remaining onion rings on top.

Variations:

Substitute 2 pkgs. (9 oz. each) frozen cut green beans for fresh.

Substitute 2 cans (15½ oz. each) cut green beans, drained. Combine with remaining ingredients; cover. Microwave at High 9 to 11 minutes, or until thoroughly heated, stirring after half the cooking time. Continue as directed above.

Hamburger & Bean Soup ▶

1 pkg. (9 oz.) frozen cut green beans
1 pkg. (9 oz.) frozen cut wax beans
¼ cup water
1 lb. ground beef
⅔ cup chopped celery
⅔ cup chopped onion
4 cups hot water
1 can (4 oz.) mushrooms, drained
1 can (16 oz.) whole tomatoes
1½ teaspoons Worcestershire sauce
1 teaspoon instant beef bouillon granules
1½ teaspoons salt
1 teaspoon parsley flakes
¼ teaspoon oregano leaves
¼ teaspoon thyme leaves
⅛ teaspoon garlic powder
⅛ teaspoon pepper

Serves 6 to 8

Place beans and water in 2-qt. casserole; cover. Microwave at High 9 to 11 minutes, or until tender, stirring after half the cooking time. Drain. Set aside.

In 5-qt. casserole combine ground beef, celery and onion. Microwave at High 4 to 6 minutes, or until meat is no longer pink, stirring to break up meat after half the cooking time. Drain all but 3 tablespoons fat.

Add beans and remaining ingredients, stirring to break apart tomatoes; cover. Microwave at High 15 to 20 minutes, or until thoroughly heated and flavors are blended, stirring 2 or 3 times during cooking. Let stand 3 to 5 minutes.

Variation:

Subsititute 1 can (15½ oz.) cut green beans and 1 can (15½ oz.) cut wax beans, drained, for frozen.

Beans: Limas & Dried Legumes

Shell beans are grown for their seeds, rather than the pods, which are tough and inedible. The varieties most often sold fresh are large limas, or butter beans, and small or baby limas.

There are many varieties of dried beans, peas and lentils. Some are popular in one locality and unknown in another, while others are identified by regional names. Legumes are an excellent source of vegetable protein. When combined with sesame seeds, rice, corn or pasta they may supply complete protein, and can be served as a main dish.

How to Select Fresh Limas & Dried Legumes

Choose well-filled, dark green pods of fresh limas. The beans should be well-developed, with a tender green or greenish-white skin. Avoid flabby pods. Look for dried legumes with bright color and uniform size. Dullness indicates long storage, a factor which will markedly prolong cooking times.

How to Store Fresh Limas & Dried Legumes

Place fresh limas in plastic bag. Refrigerate in the crisper; use within a few days. Never refrigerate dried legumes. After opening, store in an airtight container in a cool, dry place. They keep well for several months. Never combine several packages; older beans require more cooking time.

How to Rehydrate Dried Legumes

Dried legumes are usually rehydrated by soaking overnight, but can be rehydrated by microwaving. Microwave rehydration takes 1 to 2 hours, and you can add flavoring such as salt pork or bacon, green peppers, salt and seasonings during this time. Follow photo directions below.

How to Microwave Dried Legumes

Wash and sort 1 lb. beans. In a 5-qt. casserole combine with any seasonings called for in recipe. Cover with plastic wrap and casserole lid for tight seal. Microwave at High 8 to 10 minutes, or until boiling.

Let stand 1 hour, covered, or reduce power to 50% (Medium) and microwave until beans are tender. Stir several times and add hot water if needed to keep beans covered.

Serve hot as a vegetable, cold in salads, or in soups and casseroles as directed in the recipes. Additional microwaving time depends on other ingredients added and texture of bean desired.

Lima Bean Chart

Type	Amount	Microwave Time at High	Procedure
Fresh Lima Beans Large, Baby	2 cups	High: 5 min. 50% (Medium): 25-35 min.	Wash and shell. Rinse in cold water; drain. 2-qt. casserole with 1 cup water. Cover with wax paper. Stir every 5 minutes. Add hot water to cover, if needed. Let stand, covered, 5 minutes.
Frozen Lima Beans Large, Baby	10 oz. pkg.	4-7 min.	1 to 1½-qt. covered casserole with ¼ cup water and ¼ teaspoon salt. Stir once; drain.
In butter sauce	10 oz. pkg.	4½-6 min.	Flex pouch. Cut large X in one side. Place cut side down in 1-qt. casserole, or serving dish. Stir before serving.
Canned Lima Beans Large, Baby	15-16 oz.	2-3 min.	Drain all but 2 tablespoons liquid. 1-qt. covered casserole. Stir once.

◄ Orange Baked Beans

½ cup chopped onion
½ cup chopped celery
1 tablespoon butter
    or margarine
1 can (21 oz.) baked beans
¼ cup brown sugar
2 tablespoons catsup
1½ tablespoons orange juice
    concentrate
1 teaspoon prepared mustard
1 can (11 oz.) mandarin
    oranges, drained

Serves 4 to 6

In 2-qt. casserole combine onion, celery and butter. Microwave at High 2½ to 3½ minutes, or until tender.

Stir in remaining ingredients except mandarin oranges. Microwave at High 3 minutes. Mix in oranges. Microwave at High 1 to 2 minutes, or until thoroughly heated.

Variation:
Substitute recipe below for 1 can (21 oz.) baked beans.

Baked Beans

⅓ lb. Northern beans
    (about ⅔ cup)
1 teaspoon salt
3 cups hot water
3 slices bacon, cut into ½-in.
    pieces
1½ tablespoons molasses
⅛ teaspoon pepper
¼ teaspoon dry mustard

Serves 4 to 6

In 2-qt. casserole combine beans, salt and water. Cover. Microwave at High 6 to 8 minutes, or until boiling. Reduce power to 50% (Medium). Microwave 1 to 1½ hours, or until tender, stirring 4 times. Drain all but ¼ cup liquid. Add remaining ingredients. Cover.

Microwave at High 7 to 10 minutes, or until bacon is fully cooked; stir 3 to 4 times. Add water as needed to keep moist.

Northern Bean Soup

1 lb. Northern beans
8 cups water
2 teaspoons salt
1½ to 2-lb. meaty ham bone
    or 2 cups diced ham
1 large onion, chopped
½ to 1 teaspoon salt
½ teaspoon marjoram
½ teaspoon basil leaves
⅛ teaspoon pepper
1 bay leaf
2 stalks celery, cut into
    ¼-in. slices
2 large carrots, thinly sliced

Serves 6

In 5-qt. casserole combine beans, water and salt. Let stand overnight or rehydrate following photo directions on page 29.

Add ham, onion and seasonings. Cover. Microwave at High 40 minutes, or until beans are tender but not soft, stirring several times.

Remove bone from soup. Dice meat and return to casserole. Stir in vegetables. Cover.

Microwave at High 30 minutes, or until beans and vegetables are desired doneness, stirring several times during cooking. Remove bay leaf.

Variation:
Substitute 3 cans (15 oz. each) Northern beans, drained, for dry beans. Reduce water to 3½ cups. Use diced ham. Omit or reduce salt. Combine all ingredients in 5-qt. casserole. Cover. Microwave at High 35 minutes, or until vegetables are desired doneness, stirring several times during cooking.

Black Beans ▲

1 lb. black or turtle beans
8 cups water
2 teaspoons salt
1 green pepper, cut into
   chunks
3 tablespoons olive oil
1 onion, chopped
½ green pepper, chopped
3 small bay leaves
3 cloves garlic, minced
2 teaspoons oregano leaves
1 tablespoon red wine vinegar
½ teaspoon salt
¼ teaspoon black pepper

Serves 6 to 8

In 5-qt. casserole combine
beans, water, 2 teaspoons salt
and pepper chunks. Rehydrate
following photo directions, page
29. Discard pepper.

In 1-qt. casserole combine oil,
onion, green pepper, bay
leaves, garlic and oregano.
Cover. Microwave at High 4 to 5
minutes, or until vegetables are
tender. Add remaining
ingredients. Stir into beans.
Reduce power to 50%
(Medium). Cover. Microwave
1½ to 2 hours; stir every 30
minutes and add water as
needed to cover. Remove ¼
cup bean mixture, mash and
return to casserole. Microwave
45 to 60 minutes, or until
mixture is set. Serve over rice.

Split Pea & Lentil Soup

6 slices bacon, cut into 1-in.
   pieces
8 cups hot water
1 cup green split peas
1 cup lentils
1 medium onion, chopped
1 clove garlic, pressed or
   minced
1½ teaspoons salt
1 teaspoon parsley flakes
½ teaspoon oregano leaves
¼ teaspoon pepper
1 bay leaf
2 medium potatoes, peeled
   and cut into ½-in. cubes
2 medium carrots, thinly
   sliced

Serves 8

Place bacon in 5-qt. casserole.
Cover. Microwave at High 4 to 5
minutes, or until lightly browned.
Drain all but 2 tablespoons fat.
Stir in water, split peas, lentils,
onion and seasonings. Cover.
Microwave at High 40 minutes,
stirring 2 or 3 times.

Add potatoes and carrots.
Microwave, uncovered, at High,
10 to 20 minutes, or until soup
is desired thickness and
vegetables are tender, stirring
occasionally. Remove bay leaf.

Limas in Cheese Sauce

1 pkg. (10 oz.) frozen baby
   lima beans
⅓ cup chopped onion
1 tablespoon butter or
   margarine
1 tablespoon all-purpose flour
¼ teaspoon dry mustard
   Dash pepper
⅓ cup milk
1 cup grated Cheddar
   cheese, divided
1 can (4 oz.) mushroom stems
   and pieces, drained
½ cup seasoned croutons

Serves 4

Prepare lima beans as directed,
page 29. Set aside.

Place onion and butter in small
bowl. Microwave at High 1 to
1½ minutes, or until tender. Stir
in flour, seasonings, and milk.
Microwave at High 45 seconds
to 1¾ minutes, or until thickened, stirring once or twice.
Combine sauce, ¾ cup cheese,
and mushrooms, stirring until
cheese melts. Add to beans.
Sprinkle with croutons and
remaining cheese. Microwave at
High, uncovered, 1½ to 2½
minutes, or until cheese melts.

Beets

Fresh beets are available year-round, but are in greatest supply from June through October. Early beets are often sold with their tops, which can be cooked as greens. The roots must always be cooked whole and unpeeled with root ends and part of the stem uncut or the juice will "bleed".

How to Select & Store Beets

Select small to medium sized beets that are firm, smooth and deep red. Tops wilt quickly and do not indicate poor quality. Do not buy flabby, rough or shriveled beets. Large beets may be tough and woody.

Cut off all but 2 inches of tops. If they are fresh, use immediately as greens. Refrigerate roots, uncovered, in crisper and use within a week.

How to Prepare & Microwave Beets

Wash 1 lb. beets gently to avoid skin breaks. Leave root ends and 1 to 2 inches of tops intact to prevent bleeding.

Place beets in 1½-qt. casserole. Mix ½ cup water with ½ teaspoon salt until dissolved; pour over beets. Cover.

Microwave at High until fork tender, turning beets over and rotating dish every 5 minutes.

Borscht

½ lb. fresh beets, cut into
  matchsticks
2 medium carrots, thinly
  sliced
1 large onion, thinly sliced
1 medium potato, peeled
  and cut in ½-in. cubes
1½ cups shredded cabbage

1 clove garlic, minced
  or pressed
½ teaspoon salt
¼ teaspoon marjoram
⅛ teaspoon pepper
1 bay leaf
2½ cups water, divided
1 can (10½ oz.) beef broth
Dairy sour cream

Serves 4 to 6

In 3-qt. casserole, combine beets, carrots, onion, potato, cabbage, seasonings and ½ cup water. Cover. Microwave at High 14 to 17 minutes, or until vegetables are tender, stirring once or twice. Add remaining water and beef broth; cover. Microwave at High 17 to 22 minutes, or until vegetables are fork tender and flavors blended, stirring once or twice during cooking. Remove bay leaf. Top individual servings with sour cream.

Variation:

Substitute 1 can (16 oz.) shoestring beets, drained and juice reserved. Omit beets from first step, substitute reserved liquid for ½ cup of water. Reduce microwaving time to 12 minutes, stirring once or twice during cooking. Add 2 cups water, beef broth and drained beets. Re-cover. Reduce microwaving time to 10 minutes, or until beets are heated through and vegetables tender.

Orange Beets

1 lb. fresh beets or 1 can
  (16 oz.) sliced beets, drained,
  ½ cup liquid reserved
2 tablespoons brown sugar
1 tablespoon cornstarch
½ cup orange juice
½ teaspoon grated orange peel
Dash pepper
1 can (11 oz.) mandarin
  orange segments, drained

Serves 4

Prepare fresh beets as directed below. Cut into ¼-in. thick slices. Reserve liquid plus enough water to equal ½ cup. In 1½-qt. casserole combine brown sugar and cornstarch. Stir in orange juice and peel, reserved beet liquid and pepper. Microwave at High 3 to 4 minutes, or until thickened, stirring twice. Add beets. Microwave at High 2 to 2½ minutes, or until hot, stirring once. Gently mix in oranges.

Beet Chart

Type	Amount	Microwave Time at High	Procedure
Fresh Beets Whole	1 lb. (5 med.)	15-20 min.	Follow photo directions below. Let stand, covered, 3 to 5 minutes.
Canned Beets Sliced, Diced, Cuts	16 oz.	2-3 min.	1-qt. covered casserole. Drain all but 2 tablespoons liquid. Stir once.

Let stand, covered, 3 to 5 minutes, or until cool enough to handle. Slip off skins and tops. Trim root ends, if desired.

Serve beets whole, quartered or sliced. Microwave, covered, at High 1 to 2 minutes with 1 tablespoon butter.

Add lemon juice, vinegar or butter to cooked and peeled beets to enhance flavor.

Broccoli

Broccoli is a member of the cabbage family; it is milder in flavor than its relative, the cauliflower. Broccoli is available year-round; peak season is October through May. It is a good source of iron and vitamins C and A. Broccoli stalks have a tough skin which takes longer to tenderize than the buds. Peeling the stalks not only shortens cooking time, it makes broccoli more delicate in flavor.

How to Select Broccoli

Look for firm, green stalks with tightly closed, dark green or purple-green buds. Head size does not affect quality. Yellow buds or flowers indicate age and toughness.

How to Store Broccoli

Place unwashed broccoli in a plastic bag and store on refrigerator shelf. Use within a day or two.

How to Prepare & Microwave Broccoli Spears

Trim 1 in. from butt ends of 1 to 1½-lb. bunch of broccoli. Divide into spears. If desired, peel skin from 2 inches of stalks, or to where broccoli branches. Rinse in cold water.

Pour ½ cup water into 10-in. casserole or 12 × 8-in. baking dish. Arrange spears with tender heads toward center of dish. Cover with plastic wrap.

Microwave at High until stalks can be pierced with a fork, rotating dish after half the cooking time. See chart for cooking times.

How to Prepare & Microwave Broccoli Pieces

Rinse 1 to 1½-lb. bunch of broccoli. Trim off butt ends. Divide stalks in spears and peel, if desired.

Cut into 1-in. lengths. Place in 2-qt. casserole with ½ cup water; cover.

Microwave at High until pieces can be pierced with fork, stirring after half the time. See chart for cooking times.

Broccoli Chart

Type	Amount	Microwave Time at High	Procedure
Fresh Broccoli Spears	1-1½ lbs.	8-12 min.	Follow photo directions, page 35. Let stand, covered, 2 to 3 minutes.
Pieces	1-1½ lbs. (4-5 cups)	8-10 min.	Follow photo directions, page 35. Let stand, covered, 3 to 5 minutes.
Frozen Broccoli Spears, Chopped, Cuts	8-10 oz. pkg.	5-7 min.	1-qt. covered casserole with 2 tablespoons water. Stir once. Let stand, covered, 3 minutes.
In butter sauce	10 oz. pkg.	5½-7½ min.	Flex pouch. Cut large X in one side. Place cut side down in 1-qt. casserole or serving dish. Stir before serving.

Broccoli & Ham Bake

2 pkgs. (10 oz. each) frozen
  chopped broccoli
¼ cup water
1 medium onion, chopped
1 tablespoon butter or
  margarine
1 can (7½ oz.) cream of
  mushroom soup

2 cups cooked cubed ham
¾ cup shredded Cheddar
  cheese, divided
¼ cup dairy sour cream
2 teaspoons prepared mustard
⅛ teaspoon pepper
½ cup cheese flavored croutons

Serves 6 to 8

In 2-qt. casserole combine broccoli and water; cover. Microwave at High 8 to 10 minutes, or until tender. Stir once. Drain.

In 9-in. round baking dish combine onion and butter. Microwave at High 2½ to 3 minutes, or until tender, stirring once. Stir in broccoli, soup, ham, ½ cup cheese, sour cream, mustard and pepper. Cover with wax paper. Microwave at High 5 to 9 minutes, or until heated, stirring twice.

Top with croutons and remaining cheese. Microwave, uncovered, at High 1 to 2 minutes, or until cheese melts.

Toasted Almonds

1 tablespoon butter

¼ cup slivered almonds

Makes ¼ cup

Melt butter in pie plate at High 45 to 60 seconds. Stir in almonds. Microwave at High 3½ to 4½ minutes, or until lightly browned, stirring once. Let stand 5 minutes. Almonds will become darker as they stand. Serve over broccoli, sautéed celery, or cooked greens.

Spears With Lemon, Onions & Celery

1 to 1½ lbs. fresh broccoli
  or 1 pkg. (8 oz.)
  frozen broccoli spears
1 small onion, thinly sliced
  and separated into rings
¼ cup thinly sliced celery
2 tablespoons butter or
  margarine
1½ teaspoons lemon juice
½ teaspoon grated lemon
  peel
⅛ teaspoon salt
  Dash pepper
  Toasted Almonds,
  this page

Serves 4

Prepare broccoli as directed in chart. Combine onion, celery and butter in small dish or casserole. Cover. Microwave at High 2½ to 5 minutes, or until tender. Stir in lemon juice, lemon peel, salt and pepper.

Drain broccoli spears. Spoon lemon butter mixture over top. Sprinkle with toasted almonds.

Broccoli Bake ▶

2 pkgs. (8 oz. each) frozen
    broccoli spears
¼ cup water
¼ cup chopped green onion
1 tablespoon butter or
    margarine
1 pkg. (3 oz.) cream cheese

1 can (10¾ oz.) cream of
    shrimp soup
½ teaspoon grated lemon
    peel
¼ teaspoon salt
⅛ teaspoon pepper
⅛ teaspoon paprika

Serves 4 to 6

In 2-qt. casserole combine broccoli and water; cover. Microwave
at High 7 to 9 minutes, or until tender, stirring once. Drain broccoli,
arrange in 8 × 8-in. dish, alternating heads and stems.

Add onion and butter to 2-qt. casserole. Microwave at High 1 to 2
minutes, or until tender. Place cream cheese in casserole.
Microwave at High 30 to 60 seconds, or until softened. Stir in
soup, lemon peel, salt and pepper.

Pour shrimp mixture over broccoli. Sprinkle with paprika. Cover
with wax paper. Microwave at High 5 to 7 minutes, or until
thoroughly heated, rotating dish ½ turn after half the cooking time.

Broccoli Omelet ▶

1½ cups frozen chopped
    broccoli
2 tablespoons water
⅓ cup shredded Cheddar or
    Swiss cheese
4 eggs, separated
¼ cup chopped onion
¼ cup chopped green pepper

⅓ cup milk
1 teaspoon all-purpose
    flour
¼ teaspoon salt
⅛ teaspoon black pepper
1 tablespoon butter or
    margarine

Serves 4 to 6

In 1-qt. casserole combine broccoli and water, cover. Microwave
at High 4 to 6 minutes, or until fork tender, stirring after half the
cooking time. Drain. Stir in cheese. Let stand, covered.

In medium bowl combine egg yolks, onion, green pepper, milk,
flour and seasonings. Set aside. In large bowl beat egg whites until
stiff, but not dry. Fold beaten egg whites into yolk mixture until
combined. In 10-in. pie plate microwave butter at High 30 to 60
seconds, or until melted. Tilt dish to coat.

Pour egg mixture into buttered dish. Reduce power to 50%
(Medium). Microwave 7 to 10 minutes, or until set, rotating every 2
minutes and lifting edges with a spatula so uncooked portion
spreads evenly. Top with broccoli; cut into serving wedges.

Brussels Sprouts

Brussels sprouts are miniature cabbages which go well with any meat dish, and can be served with family or party fare. They are available from October through March.

How to Select Brussels Sprouts

Look for firm sprouts with tight, green leaves. Avoid puffy or soft sprouts with loose leaves. Wilted or yellow leaves indicate over-ripe sprouts. Place in sealed container; store in refrigerator. Do not wash until ready to use. Use as soon as possible.

How to Prepare & Microwave Brussels Sprouts

Wash 1 lb. of sprouts. Remove loose leaves. Trim stems; cut a cross in each to speed cooking. Place in 1½-qt. casserole.

Add ¼ cup water; cover. Microwave at High until fork tender, stirring once. See chart for cooking times.

Brussels Sprouts Chart

Type	Amount	Microwave Time at High	Procedure
Fresh Brussels Sprouts			
Whole	1 lb. (4 cups)	4-8 min.	Follow photo directions. Let stand, covered, 3 minutes.
Frozen Brussels Sprouts			
Whole	10 oz. pkg.	5-7 min.	1-qt. covered casserole with 2 tablespoons water. Let stand 3 minutes.
In butter sauce	10 oz. pkg.	5-7 min.	Flex pouch. Cut large X in one side. Place cut side down in 1-qt. casserole. Let stand 3 minutes. Stir before serving.

Cabbage

Versatile cabbages are plentiful year-round. They are a rich source of vitamin C, high in fiber and low in sodium and calories. To preserve nutrients, microwave just until tender. Long cooking develops strong odor and flavor. Green, red and savoy cabbage may be cooked in bouillon, served with butter, salt and pepper, or seasoned with caraway. Green or savoy cabbage can be creamed or topped with cheese sauce.

Chinese cabbage, also called Napa or celery cabbage, is cylindrical in shape and milder in flavor than round cabbages. Use in oriental dishes or dress with melted butter, bacon, sour cream, Parmesan cheese or lemon juice.

Tender, sweet-tasting bok choy looks like Swiss chard. The name means "white vegetable", and both stalks and leaves are used in Chinese dishes.

How to Select Green, Red & Savoy Cabbage

Choose green or red cabbage heads which are solid and heavy for their size. New cabbage is less firm than fall and winter varieties, and green cabbage is more nutritious than white. Crinkly Savoy cabbage has pale green to yellow green leaves formed in a looser, lighter head similar to Iceberg lettuce.

Select firm heads with "tight" leaves. Avoid soft spots and decayed or damaged leaves. Separation of leaves from central stem indicates age.

How to Select Chinese Cabbage & Bok Choy

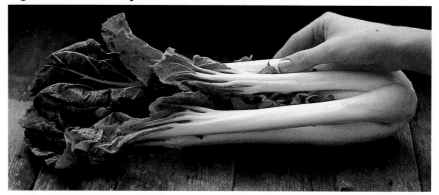

Buy long or squat heads of Chinese cabbage which are compact with very crisp green leaves. Fall and winter harvests are mildest in flavor.

Look for bok choy with firm, very white stalks and shiny dark green leaves. The heart is considered a great delicacy and is sometimes sold separately. Leaves and stalks are both tender and may be microwaved together.

How to Store Cabbage

Store cabbage whole or in large pieces; small pieces wilt quickly. Refrigerate cabbage in a plastic bag to provide humidity.

Wash and trim cabbage just before using to prevent mold or discoloration during storage. Use new cabbage, available in spring and summer, Savoy, Chinese and bok choy quickly. Fall and winter types are grown for storage and keep one to two weeks.

How to Prepare Green, Red & Savoy Cabbage for Microwaving

Cut 1-lb. cabbage into 4 wedges. Line up in 12 × 8-in. dish or arrange like wheel spokes in 10-in. casserole. Add liquid; cover with plastic wrap.

Shred cabbage into ¼-in. wide pieces. A 1-lb. head of green or red cabbage makes 3½ to 4½ cups, while ½-lb. Savoy cabbage makes 7 to 8 cups. Place shreds and liquid in a tightly covered casserole. To preserve the color of red cabbage, cut with a stainless steel knife and add lemon juice or vinegar.

How to Prepare Chinese Cabbage & Bok Choy for Microwaving

Wash bok choy carefully. Cut stalks into ⅛-in. slices and leaves into ½-in. strips.

Trim and wash 1½-lb. Chinese cabbage just before cooking. Remove bottom inch and expose stem. Cut leaves and stalks crosswise into 1-in. strips, discarding core.

Cabbage Chart

Type	Amount	Microwave Time at High	Procedure
Fresh Cabbage Green, Red, Savoy	1 lb. (4 wedges)	12½-15½ min.	12 × 8-in. covered dish. ¼ cup water. 2 teaspoons vinegar for red. Rearrange cabbage and rotate dish once. Let stand, covered, 2 to 3 minutes.
Green, shredded	1 lb.	7½-13½ min.	1-qt. covered casserole. 2 tablespoons water. Stir once. Let stand, covered, 3 minutes.
Red, shredded	1 lb.	7-13 min.	1½-qt. covered casserole. ¼ cup water, 2 teaspoons vinegar, 2 teaspoons sugar. Stir once. Let stand, covered, 3 minutes.
Savoy, shredded	½ lb.	9-11 min.	2-qt. covered casserole. ¼ cup water. Stir once. Let stand, covered, 3 minutes.
Chinese, chopped	1½ lbs.	9½-11 min.	3-qt. covered casserole. ¼ cup water. Stir once. Let stand, covered, 3 minutes.

◄ Cabbage & Noodles

4 cups shredded cabbage
1 small onion, thinly sliced
   and separated into rings
3 tablespoons butter or
   margarine
½ teaspoon poppy seeds
½ teaspoon salt
   Dash pepper
2 cups cooked medium-sized
   egg noodles

Serves 4 to 6

In 2-qt. casserole combine all ingredients except egg noodles. Cover. Microwave at High 5 to 6 minutes, or until cabbage is tender, stirring after half the cooking time. Stir in noodles.

Cabbage-Bacon Sauté

6 slices bacon
3 cups shredded green
   cabbage
1 cup shredded red cabbage
1 tablespoon sugar
½ teaspoon salt
   Dash pepper
2 tablespoons vinegar

Serves 4

Arrange bacon on rack in 12 × 8-in. dish. Cover with paper towel. Microwave at High 6 minutes. Let stand 3 to 5 minutes. Crumble bacon. Remove rack from dish and discard all but 3 tablespoons fat.

Add crumbled bacon, cabbage, sugar, seasonings and vinegar to dish. Cover with plastic wrap. Microwave at High 5 minutes, or until cabbage is tender, stirring after half the cooking time.

Bok Choy Sauté

3 large stalks bok choy
2 tablespoons butter or
   margarine
2 tablespoons soy sauce
¼ teaspoon garlic powder
1 teaspoon sugar
1 small carrot, cut into
   matchsticks
8 oz. fresh mushrooms,
   sliced

Serves 4 to 6

Slice bok choy stalks into ⅛-in. slices and leaves into ½-in. strips. In 2-qt. casserole melt butter at High 1 to 1½ minutes.

Add soy sauce, garlic powder and sugar. Stir in carrots, mushrooms and bok choy. Cover.

Microwave at High 4½ to 5½ minutes, or until tender-crisp, stirring after half the time.

Creamy Sauerkraut

1 tablespoon butter or
   margarine
1 tablespoon all-purpose flour
¼ teaspoon salt
   Dash pepper
½ cup half and half
½ cup milk
1 can (16 oz.) sauerkraut,
   rinsed and drained
1 teaspoon caraway seeds
½ teaspoon sugar

Serves 4

In 1 to 1½-qt. casserole melt butter at High 30 to 60 seconds. Stir in flour, salt and pepper. Blend in half and half and milk. Microwave at High 4 to 6 minutes, or until bubbly and slightly thickened, stirring every minute.

Stir in sauerkraut, caraway seeds and sugar. Microwave at High 1 to 2 minutes, or until heated through.

Stuffed Cabbage Head ▶

1 large cabbage
½ cup water
½ lb. ground beef
½ lb. ground pork
1 medium apple, cored
   and chopped
1 medium onion, chopped
¼ cup dry bread crumbs
1 cup cooked rice
1 egg
2 teaspoons Worcestershire
   sauce
1 teaspoon salt
¼ teaspoon allspice
⅛ teaspoon pepper

Serves 6

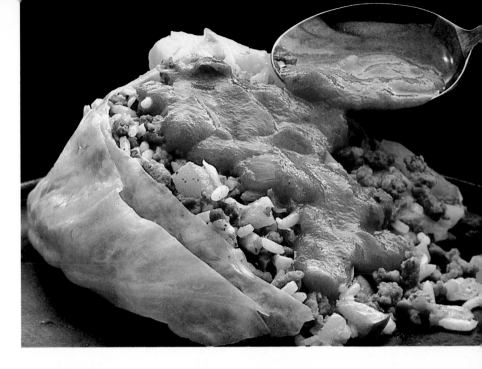

How to Microwave Stuffed Cabbage Head

Place cabbage and water in 5-qt. casserole. Cover. Microwave at High 6 to 9 minutes, or until outer leaves are supple. Drain. Let cool.

Place cool cabbage on 2 crisscrossed sheets of plastic wrap. Gently pull back outer leaves. Cut out heart, leaving outer leaves attached to stem.

Chop heart finely. Combine in 2-qt. casserole with ground beef, pork, apple and onion.

Microwave at High 4 to 6 minutes, or until meat is no longer pink, stirring to break up after half the cooking time. Drain well. Add remaining ingredients to meat mixture.

Place cabbage leaves and plastic wrap in a deep bowl. Mold three-fourths of meat mixture into center. Cover with one or two leaves. Press extra meat mixture around edges, folding leaves over it.

Secure plastic wrap tightly around cabbage. Microwave at High 4 to 6 minutes, or until cabbage yields to light pressure. Remove from bowl, unwrap and serve in wedges. Serve with Tomato Sauce, page 111.

Carrots

Carrots are available year-round. Baby carrots with tender skins can be scrubbed and cooked whole. Larger carrots should be peeled or scraped, then cut up for faster, more even microwaving. Older carrots have a tough, woody core. Halve them lengthwise, then pry out the pale core with a sharp knife. The outer portion can be cut up and microwaved like young, tender carrots.

Vary the appearance of carrots by cutting them in different ways. They may be cut into 2-in. lengths, julienned, diced or grated. Slice carrots crosswise into rounds or on the diagonal for oval shapes.

How to Select & Store Carrots

Look for firm, well-formed, smooth carrots with bright orange to orange-red color. Small to medium carrots offer best flavor.

Avoid flabby, shriveled or soft carrots and those with large green areas. Yellow tops on bunched carrots or green shoots on trimmed carrots indicate age.

Trim tops to save space. Do not wash until ready to use. Good quality carrots, stored in plastic bag and refrigerated, keep for several months.

Carrot Chart

Type	Amount	Microwave Time at High	Procedure
Fresh Carrots			
Baby, whole	12 oz.	6-8 min.	1-qt. covered casserole with 2 tablespoons water. Stir once. Let stand, covered, 3 minutes.
Cuts, 2-in.	10-12 med.	6-8 min.	1-qt. covered casserole with 2 tablespoons water. Stir once. Let stand, covered, 3 minutes.
Slices, ¼-in.	2 cups	4-7 min.	1-qt. covered casserole with 2 tablespoons water. Stir once. Let stand, covered, 3 minutes.
Frozen Carrots			
Baby, whole	16 oz.	6½-8½ min.	1-qt. covered casserole with 2 tablespoons water. Stir once. Let stand, covered, 3 minutes.
Crinkle cut	2 cups	4-7 min.	1-qt. covered casserole with 2 tablespoons water. Stir once. Let stand, covered, 3 minutes.
In butter sauce	10 oz. pkg.	5-6 min.	Flex pouch. Cut large X in one side. Place cut side down in 1-qt. casserole or serving dish. Stir before serving.
Canned Carrots			
Cuts, Slices, Diced	16 oz.	2½-3 min.	Drain all but 2 tablespoons liquid. 1-qt. covered casserole. Stir once.

Glazed Baby Carrots ▲

12 oz. fresh baby carrots,
   scrubbed
2 tablespoons water

Glaze:

1½ tablespoons butter or
   margarine
1½ tablespoons brown sugar
 ¼ teaspoon cinnamon
 ⅛ teaspoon ground cloves
 ⅛ teaspoon salt
 2 tablespoons chopped
   pecans, optional

Serves 4

Prepare carrots as directed,
page 45. Set aside.

In small bowl or 1-cup measure
microwave butter at High 30 to
45 seconds, or until melted. Stir
in brown sugar, cinnamon, cloves
and salt. Drain carrots. Pour
glaze over and stir to coat.
Microwave at High 20 seconds
to melt brown sugar, if needed.
Stir. If desired, garnish with
chopped pecans.

Variation:

Substitute 16 oz. frozen whole
baby carrots for the fresh.

Celery Carrots

6 medium carrots,
   sliced ¼ in. thick
2 stalks celery, thinly sliced
2 tablespoons water
½ teaspoon salt
1 can (16 oz.) stewed
   tomatoes, drained, ¼ cup
   liquid reserved
2 tablespoons all-purpose
   flour
4 slices bacon, microwaved
   and crumbled
½ teaspoon sugar
   Dash pepper

Serves 4 to 6

Combine carrots, celery, water
and salt in 1½ to 2-qt.
casserole. Cover. Microwave at
High 7 to 9 minutes, or until fork
tender, stirring after half the
cooking time. Do not drain.

In small dish blend ¼ cup
reserved tomato liquid and flour
until smooth. Add to casserole.

Stir in remaining ingredients.
Cover; microwave at High 3 to 4
minutes, or until thickened,
stirring once during cooking.

Carrots With Onion, ▲
Sour Cream & Dill

6 medium carrots, peeled
   and cut into julienne strips
2 tablespoons water
½ teaspoon salt, divided
¼ cup chopped green onion
¼ cup dairy sour cream
1 tablespoon packed brown
   sugar
¼ teaspoon dill weed

Serves 4 to 6

In 1½ to 2-qt. casserole
combine carrots, water and ¼
teaspoon salt. Cover.
Microwave at High 7 to 8
minutes, or until fork tender,
stirring after half the time. Drain
and reserve 1 tablespoon liquid.

Stir remaining ingredients and
reserved liquid into carrots.
Cover. Microwave at High 1 to 2
minutes, or until green onion is
tender-crisp.

Carrots With Chicken Broth & Rosemary

1 lb. carrots, peeled and
    sliced ¼ in. thick
¼ cup water

Broth:

⅓ cup water
2 teaspoons cornstarch
2 teaspoons instant chicken
    bouillon granules
1 teaspoon chives
½ teaspoon whole rosemary,
    crushed
 Dash pepper

Serves 4 to 6

In 1½ to 2-qt. casserole combine carrots and ¼ cup water. Cover; microwave at High 8 to 10 minutes, or until fork tender, stirring once during cooking. Do not drain.

Mix ⅓ cup water and cornstarch in 1-cup measure until smooth. Add remaining ingredients. Stir into carrots. Cover; microwave at High 3 to 4 minutes, or until thickened, stirring after half the time.

Carrot Cake ▲

¾ cup all-purpose flour
½ cup sugar
¼ cup packed brown sugar
1 teaspoon baking soda
½ teaspoon salt
1 teaspoon cinnamon
½ teaspoon nutmeg

½ cup vegetable oil
1¼ cups shredded carrots
2 eggs
¼ cup finely chopped nuts
¼ cup raisins
    Cream Cheese Frosting,
    below

Makes 8 × 8-in. cake

Place all ingredients except frosting in mixing bowl. Blend at low speed; then beat at medium speed 2 minutes. Spread batter in 8 × 8-in. baking dish.

Elevate baking dish on inverted saucer. Microwave at 50% (Medium) 6 minutes, rotating ¼ turn after first 3 minutes. Increase power to High. Microwave 4 to 6 minutes, or until toothpick inserted in center comes out clean, rotating dish ¼ turn once during cooking. Let stand directly on countertop 5 to 10 minutes. Cool and frost with cream cheese frosting.

Cream Cheese Frosting

1 pkg. (3 oz.) cream cheese
2 tablespoons butter or
    margarine

1½ to 2 cups confectioners'
    sugar

Frosts 8 × 8-in. cake

Combine cream cheese and butter in mixing bowl. Microwave at High 10 to 20 seconds, or until softened. Blend well. Beat in sugar until of spreading consistency. Spread on cooled cake.

Cauliflower

Cauliflower is available all year, with best supply from September through January. The size of the head does not affect quality. Standing time is important when microwaving cauliflower, especially a whole head. It allows stems to tenderize without overcooking the flowerets. If you separate the cauliflower into flowerets, halve or quarter large ones to make uniform pieces.

How to Select Cauliflower

Choose clean heads with compact, firm, white or slightly creamy-white flowerets. Any leaves should be fresh and green. Avoid loose, open flower clusters, mold specks or bruised areas.

How to Store Cauliflower

Keep in original wrapper or cover loosely with plastic wrap. Refrigerate on the shelf up to several days.

How to Prepare & Microwave Whole Cauliflower

Break off outer leaves and trim stem close to base of a 1-lb. head of cauliflower. Wash in cool water; shake off excess.

Wrap head in plastic wrap; place on paper plate with sealed edges down. Microwave at High 3 minutes. Turn cauliflower over.

Microwave at High until head is flexible and floweret stems are almost fork tender. See chart for cooking times.

48

Cheesy Cauliflower

1 medium head cauliflower
    (about 1 lb.)
4 oz. fresh mushrooms, sliced
1 tablespoon butter or
    margarine
1 tablespoon all-purpose flour
¼ teaspoon dry mustard
¼ teaspoon salt
    Dash pepper
1 teaspoon fresh snipped
    parsley
½ cup milk
1 cup shredded Cheddar
    cheese
⅓ cup dairy sour cream

Serves 4 to 6

Prepare and microwave
cauliflower following photo
directions on opposite page.

Combine mushrooms and butter
in 1 to 1½-qt. casserole.
Microwave at High 1½ to 2
minutes, or until mushrooms are
tender, stirring after 1 minute.
Blend in flour and seasonings.
Stir in milk. Microwave at High
1½ to 3 minutes, or until
thickened, stirring every minute.
Mix in cheese. Microwave at
High 15 seconds to melt, if
necessary. Blend in sour cream.
Serve over cauliflower.

Variation:
Substitute fresh snipped chives
for parsley. Garnish with
Toasted Almonds, page 36.

Cauliflower & Peas ► in Cream Sauce

2 cups fresh cauliflowerets
    or 1 pkg. (10 oz.)
    frozen cauliflower
1 cup frozen peas
2 tablespoons water

Sauce:
¼ cup chopped onion
1 tablespoon butter or
    margarine
1 tablespoon all-purpose flour
¼ cup half and half
¼ cup water
1 tablespoon chopped
    pimiento
½ teaspoon parsley flakes
½ teaspoon instant chicken
    bouillon granules
⅛ teaspoon salt
    Dash pepper

Serves 4 to 6

In 1 to 1½-qt. casserole combine cauliflowerets, peas and
water. Cover. Microwave at
High 6 to 8 minutes, or until fork
tender, stirring after half the
time. Let stand, covered.

Place onion and butter in 2-cup
measure. Microwave at High 1
to 1½ minutes, or until onion is
tender. Stir in flour. Add remaining ingredients. Microwave at
High 1½ to 2 minutes, or until
thickened, stirring every minute.
Drain vegetables. Pour sauce
over and stir to coat.

Cauliflower Chart

Type	Amount	Microwave Time at High	Procedure
Fresh Cauliflower			
Whole head	1 lb.	5½-7½ min.	Follow photo directions. Let stand, covered, 3 minutes.
Flowerets	2 cups	4-7 min.	1½-qt. covered casserole with ¼ cup water. Stir once. Let stand, covered, 2 to 3 minutes.
Frozen Cauliflower			
Flowerets	10 oz. pkg.	5-7 min.	1-qt. covered casserole with 2 tablespoons water. Stir once. Let stand, covered, 3 minutes.

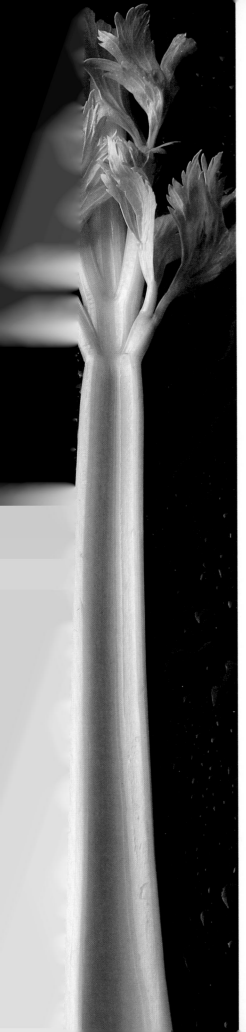

Celery

Celery is plentiful all year. Some may be bleached white, but most celery is the dark or light green Pascal variety. The whole stalk is edible, including the leaves, which are delicious for flavoring salads, soups, casseroles and sauces.

How to Select & Store Celery

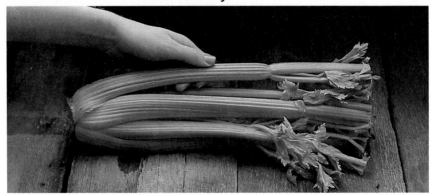

Choose glossy stalks of medium length and thickness, which are crisp enough to snap easily. Look for a well-formed heart and stems which feel smooth on the inside. If stems feel rough or puffy, or if the cut ends appear overly porous, celery may be soft and pithy. Avoid limp celery, wilted leaflets or seed stems. Refrigerate celery, unwashed, in its store wrap or a perforated plastic bag. It keeps well for a week or more.

How to Prepare & Microwave Celery

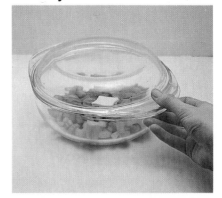

Wash celery; pull off coarse strings. Slice ⅛ to ¼ in. thick, to make 2 cups. Combine in 1½-qt. casserole with 2 tablespoons butter or water. Cover.

Microwave at High 5 to 8 minutes, or until fork tender, stirring after 4 minutes. Let stand, covered, 3 minutes.

Celery Victor ▲

4 cups sliced celery
  ½-in. diagonal pieces
1½ cups sliced fresh
  mushrooms
1 small onion, chopped
2 tablespoons olive oil
2 teaspoons lemon juice
⅔ cup water
1 teaspoon instant chicken
  bouillon granules
1 teaspoon cornstarch
½ teaspoon parsley flakes
1 teaspoon basil leaves
⅛ teaspoon pepper
1 bay leaf

Serves 4 to 6

Place celery, mushrooms, onion, olive oil and lemon juice in 2-qt. casserole. Set aside.

In 2-cup measure combine water, bouillon, cornstarch and seasonings. Microwave at High 1½ to 2½ minutes, or until bubbly and slightly thickened, stirring after half the time.

Add to celery mixture. Cover. Microwave at High 6 to 8 minutes, or until celery is tender-crisp, stirring after half the cooking time. Chill several hours before serving.

Celery Soup

2 slices bacon, cut into ¾-in.
  pieces
2 cups thinly sliced celery
¼ cup chopped onion
1 cup water, divided
⅓ cup all purpose flour*
1 teaspoon chervil
½ teaspoon salt
⅛ teaspoon pepper
¼ teaspoon celery seed
2 cups milk
½ cup half and half or whipping
  cream

Makes 1-qt.

Place bacon in 2-qt. casserole. Cover. Microwave at High 2 to 2½ minutes, or until browned.

Add celery, onion and ¼ cup water to casserole. Cover. Microwave at High 5 to 8 minutes, or until tender, stirring after half the cooking time.

Mix in flour and seasonings. Blend in remaining water and milk. Microwave, uncovered, at High 8 to 11 minutes, or until thickened, stirring 3 or 4 times. Stir in cream.

*For thinner soup reduce flour to ¼ cup.

Sautéed Celery With ▲ Toasted Almonds

8 stalks celery, cut diagonally
  into 1 to 1½-in. pieces
⅓ cup chopped green onion
2 tablespoons butter or
  margarine
  Dash garlic powder
  Dash pepper
½ teaspoon sugar
¼ teaspoon salt
  Toasted Almonds, page 36

Serves 4 to 6

In 1½-qt. casserole combine celery, onion, butter, garlic powder and pepper. Cover. Microwave at High 6 minutes, or until tender-crisp, stirring after half the cooking time.

Stir in sugar and salt. Mix in toasted almonds.

Variation: Omit toasted almonds and stir in sliced pimiento or bacon bits.

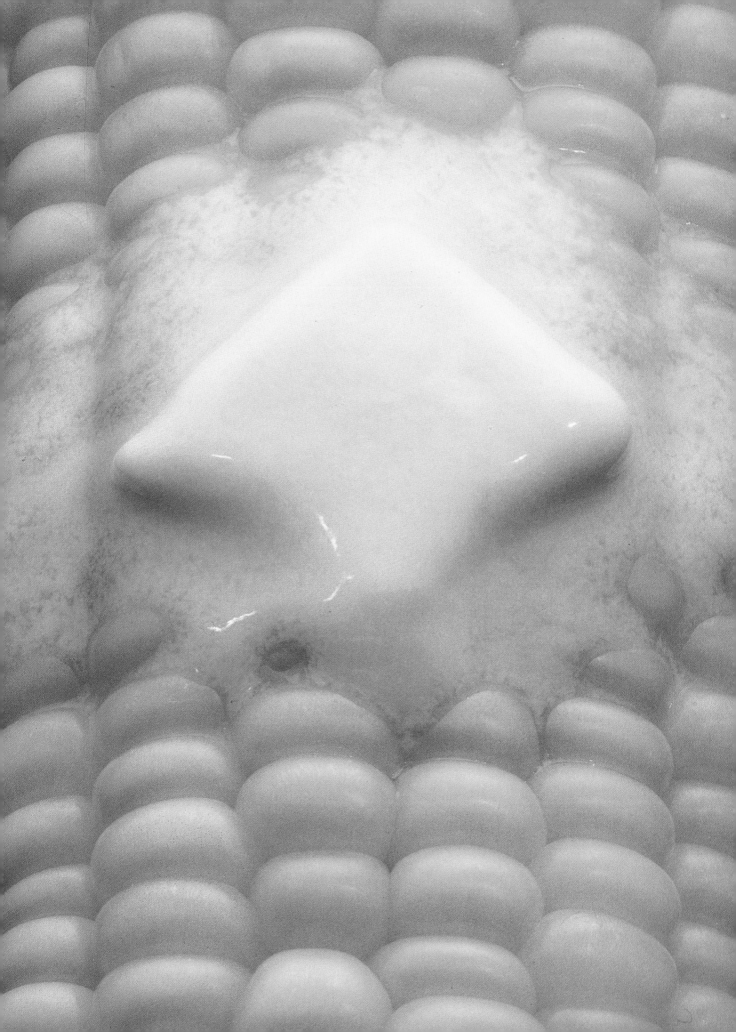

Corn

Microwaving enhances the flavor and nutrition of corn. For best flavor, microwave as soon after picking as possible, right in the husk, which provides a natural cover. Individual ears of husked corn may be wrapped in plastic and cooked like corn in the husk, or placed in a tightly covered dish. Be sure to leave space between the ears and allow standing time. Do not salt before cooking or corn will toughen. The peak season for corn is May through September.

How to Store Corn

Use immediately for best flavor. The natural sugar in corn begins to convert to starch within a few hours after picking. If storage is necessary, wrap unhusked ears in plastic wrap and refrigerate.

How to Select Corn

Choose ears with fresh green husks, moist stem ends, and silk free from decay or worm damage. Avoid yellowed or dried husks.

Look for plump, tender, milky kernels in close rows extending to the tip of the ear. Kernels should be firm enough to puncture easily with slight pressure. Immature corn has very soft, small kernels. Large or dark yellow kernels indicate age.

How to Microwave Corn in Husk

Arrange ears in the husk on oven floor with space between. No preparation is needed. Microwave at High; rotate and rearrange during cooking.

Cover tightly during standing. Husk corn after standing. Using paper napkin, hold corn with tip pointing down. Pull back leaves carefully to avoid steam. Grasp silk in other hand and pull sharply.

How to Microwave Corn on the Cob

Wrap individual ears of fresh husked corn in plastic before placing them in oven.

Or arrange fresh or frozen ears in baking dish, with space between. Add water as directed in chart; cover with plastic wrap.

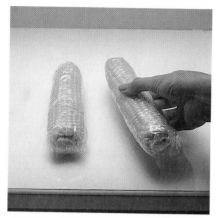

Place individual ears or dish of corn in oven. Microwave at High following times in chart.

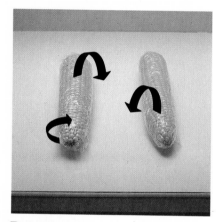

Rearrange 2 ears after half the cooking time, turning them over so tips of ears are placed in a different part of the oven.

Turn over and rearrange 3 or more ears every 4 minutes, moving them from side to center and back to front of the oven.

Let fresh ears stand 5 minutes and frozen ears 3 minutes.

How to Microwave Corn Kernels

Place canned or frozen whole kernel corn in dish with 2 tablespoons liquid. For canned corn, use 2 tablespoons of liquid from can. Cover.

Microwave at High, stirring after half the cooking time. Let frozen corn stand 3 minutes.

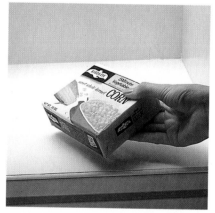

Defrost corn for recipes by placing package in oven. Microwave at High 2 to 3 minutes, turning over and flexing box after half the time. Let stand 5 minutes.

Corn Chart

Type	Amount	Microwave Time at High	Procedure
Fresh Corn on the Cob			
In Husk (7-8 oz. each)	1 2	3-5 min. 4-9 min.	Follow photo directions, page 53. Turn over, rearrange after half the time. Let stand 5 minutes.
	3 4	9-12 min. 10-17 min.	Follow photo directions, page 53. Turn over, rearrange every 4 minutes. Let stand 5 minutes
Husked (7-8 oz. each)	1 2	2-5 min. 4½-10 min.	Follow photo directions. Wrap in plastic wrap or tightly covered dish with ¼ cup water. Turn over, rearrange every 4 minutes. Let stand 5 minutes.
	3 4	6-12 min. 7½-16 min.	Follow photo directions. Wrap in plastic wrap or tightly covered dish with ¼ cup water. Turn over, rearrange every 4 minutes. Let stand 5 minutes.
Frozen Corn			
Small ears	1 2	2½-3 min. 5½-7½ min.	Follow photo directions. Tightly covered dish with 2 tablespoons water. Turn over and rearrange after half the time. Let stand 3 minutes.
	4 8	5-8 min. 10-12½ min.	Follow photo directions. Tightly covered dish with 2 tablespoons water. Turn over and rearrange every 4 minutes. Let stand 3 minutes.
Whole kernel	10 oz. pkg (2 cups)	4-6 min.	Follow photo directions. 1-qt. covered casserole with 2 tablespoons water. Stir once. Let stand 3 minutes.
In butter sauce or Cream style	10 oz. pkg	4½-5 min.	Flex pouch. Cut large X in one side. Place cut side down in 1-qt. covered casserole or serving dish. Stir before serving.
Canned Corn			
Whole kernel	10 oz.	2-3 min.	Follow photo directions. Drain all but 2 tablespoons liquid. 1-qt. covered casserole. Stir once.
Cream style	16 oz.	2½-4 min.	1-qt. covered casserole. Stir once during cooking and before serving.

Corn, Egg & Swiss Bake

2 pkgs. (10 oz. each) frozen
   whole kernel corn
2 tablespoons water
¼ cup chopped green onion
1 cup shredded Swiss
   cheese, divided
1 can (5⅓ oz.) evaporated
   milk
½ cup soft bread crumbs
1 egg, slightly beaten
½ teaspoon salt
   Dash pepper

             Serves 6 to 8

Combine corn and water in
2-qt. casserole; cover. Microwave at High 6 minutes. Stir in
onion; cover. Microwave at
High 1½ to 2 minutes, or until
corn is hot and onion is tender.

Drain well. Stir in ¾ cup
cheese and remaining ingredients. Microwave uncovered
at High 3 minutes. Reduce
power to 50% (Medium). Microwave 7 to 13 minutes, or
until almost set, rotating dish
½ turn after half the time.

Sprinkle with remaining
cheese. Microwave at 50%
(Medium) 1 to 2 minutes, or
until cheese melts. Let stand
1 to 2 minutes.

Creole Corn ▲

⅓ cup chopped celery
⅓ cup chopped green pepper
2 teaspoons olive oil
1 pkg. (10 oz.) frozen whole
   kernel corn, defrosted
   or 1 can (12 or 16 oz.),
   drained
1 can (8 oz.) tomato sauce
1 can (4 oz.) mushroom stems
   and pieces, drained
1 tomato, peeled and
   chopped
2 teaspoons brown sugar
½ teaspoon onion powder
⅛ teaspoon garlic powder
⅛ teaspoon salt
   Dash black pepper
   Dash cayenne pepper
1 tablespoon catsup

             Serves 6 to 8

In 1½-qt. casserole combine
celery, green pepper and oil.
Cover. Microwave at High 2 to
2½ minutes, or until tender.

Stir in corn and remaining ingredients. Cover. Microwave at
High 2 to 3 minutes, or until
thoroughly heated, stirring once.

Corn Relish

⅔ cup sugar
1 tablespoon cornstarch
½ teaspoon dry mustard
¼ teaspoon salt
   Dash cayenne pepper
⅓ cup vinegar
1 can (12 or 16 oz.) whole
   kernel corn, drained,
   or 1 pkg. (10 oz.) frozen,
   defrosted
1 small onion, chopped
2 tablespoons chopped green
   pepper
1 tablespoon chopped
   pimiento

            Makes 3 cups

In 1 to 1½-qt. casserole combine sugar, cornstarch and
seasonings. Stir in vinegar.
Microwave at High 2 to 4
minutes or until boiling and
slightly thickened.

Mix in remaining ingredients.
Cool; refrigerate 6 hours, or
overnight to blend flavors.

Variation:
For sweeter relish increase
sugar to 1 cup.

Seasoned Kernels

1 pkg. (10 oz.) frozen whole
   kernel corn
1 tablespoon water
1 tablespoon butter or
   margarine
1 teaspoon chopped chives
¼ teaspoon basil
¼ teaspoon sugar
⅛ teaspoon salt
   Dash pepper

            Serves 3 to 4

Combine corn, water and butter in 1-qt. casserole. Cover.
Microwave at High 4 to 5 minutes, or until butter melts and
corn is defrosted. Stir in remaining ingredients. Re-cover.
Microwave at High 1 to 2 minutes, or until hot throughout.

Corn Chowder

¼ lb. ground pork sausage
½ cup chopped onion
4 cups milk, divided
¼ cup all-purpose flour
1½ teaspoons parsley flakes
1 teaspoon salt
⅛ teaspoon pepper
1 egg, slightly beaten
1 can (16 oz.) cream style
   corn
1 can (12 or 16 oz.) whole
   kernel corn, drained
   Paprika

Serves 6 to 8

In 3-qt. casserole combine sausage and onion. Microwave at High 3 minutes, or until meat is no longer pink, stirring after half the cooking time.

Blend 1 cup milk and flour until smooth. Add to sausage with seasonings. Microwave at High 2 to 5½ minutes, or until thick and bubbly, stirring 3 or 4 times during cooking. Stir in remaining milk.

Add small amount of hot milk mixture to egg. Return to casserole. Stir in cream style and whole kernel corn. Microwave at High 7 to 12 minutes, or until slightly thickened, stirring once during cooking.

Sprinkle individual servings with paprika, if desired.

Variation:
Substitute 6 strips bacon cut into ½-in. pieces for sausage and add ¼ cup chopped green pepper with onion. Microwave at High 3 minutes, or until vegetables are tender and bacon is lightly browned. Drain all but 2 tablespoons fat. Substitute 1 can (12 oz.) Mexican style corn for whole kernel corn.

Variation:
Substitute 3 tablespoons butter or margarine for sausage (gives chowder milder flavor). Microwave at High 2 minutes, or until onion is tender.

Spiced Corn Muffins ▲

⅔ cup all-purpose flour
⅓ cup whole wheat flour
⅓ cup corn meal
1 teaspoon baking soda
1 teaspoon baking powder
1 teaspoon pumpkin pie spice
½ teaspoon salt
3 eggs
⅔ cup vegetable oil
⅔ cup brown sugar
1 tablespoon light
   molasses
1 can (12 or 16 oz.) whole
   kernel corn, drained
½ cup finely chopped pecans

Makes 1½ to 2 dozen muffins

Combine flours, corn meal, baking soda, baking powder, pie spice and salt in bowl. Set aside. Beat eggs, oil, brown sugar and molasses until smooth; stir in corn. Add dry ingredients, stirring until moistened.

Line a microwave cupcake dish or each of 6 custard cups with two paper liners. Fill cups half full. Sprinkle with pecans.

Arrange custard cups (if used) in a ring. Microwave 6 muffins at High, 2 to 2¾ minutes, or until tops spring back when lightly touched, rotating muffins after half the time. Remove from cups to wire rack immediately. Repeat with remaining batter.

Eggplant

Eggplants are picked when they are immature and firm with soft seeds. Mature eggplants with soft flesh and tough seeds will have poor flavor. The versatile eggplant may be served hot or cold, stuffed, by itself or in combination with other vegetables. Eggplants are available year-round, but are most plentiful in August and September.

How to Select Eggplant

Choose small eggplants, 3 to 6 inches in diameter, which are firm and heavy for their size. Look for green caps and smooth, shiny skins free of brown spots, scars or cuts. Avoid dull, wrinkled, pitted or even slightly soft eggplants, which may taste bitter.

How to Store Eggplant

Refrigerate eggplant uncovered in the crisper, and use as soon as possible. During refrigeration, eggplants soften and develop brown spots and bitter flavor within a few days.

How to Prepare & Microwave Eggplant Cubes

Prepare 1½-lb. eggplant just before cooking; it darkens when cut. Wash eggplant and remove cap. Peel with sharp knife or leave skin on for color contrast. Cut into ¾-in. cubes.

Place cubes in 2-qt. casserole with 2 tablespoons butter; cover. Microwave at High 7 to 10 minutes, or until tender, stirring every 2 minutes. Let stand, covered, 3 to 5 minutes.

Serve sprinkled with Parmesan cheese, snipped chives or parsley. Season with salt and pepper, garlic, oregano, thyme, rosemary, allspice, nutmeg or curry powder.

Eggplant Parmesan ▶

½ cup chopped onion
1 tablespoon butter or
  margarine
1 can (15 oz.) tomato sauce
2 teaspoons brown sugar
½ teaspoon oregano leaves
  Dash pepper
1 egg, slightly beaten

1 tablespoon milk
6 to 8 slices medium eggplant,
  unpeeled, ¾-in. thick
½ cup fine dry bread crumbs
1 cup grated mozzarella
  cheese, divided
¼ cup grated Parmesan
  cheese

Serves 4

Place onion and butter in 1 to 1½-qt. casserole; cover. Microwave at High 2 to 3 minutes, or until tender. Stir in tomato sauce, brown sugar, oregano and pepper. Re-cover. Microwave at High 3 minutes. Stir. Reduce power to 50% (Medium). Microwave 5 to 7 minutes, or until hot and flavors are blended, stirring after half the cooking time. Set sauce aside.

Combine egg and milk. Dip eggplant slices in egg mixture, then coat with bread crumbs. Place in 12 × 8-in. dish in single layer, overlapping edges, if necessary. Cover dish with wax paper.

Microwave at High 11 to 15 minutes, or until eggplant skin is fork tender, rearranging slices and rotating dish ½ turn after half the cooking time. Sprinkle three-fourths of mozzarella cheese over top. Spoon sauce over. Top with remaining cheeses. Microwave at High 1½ to 2 minutes, or until cheeses melt.

Stuffed Eggplant ▶

½ lb. ground pork sausage
1 medium eggplant
1 cup sliced fresh mushrooms
½ cup chopped green pepper
¼ cup chopped onion
1 clove garlic, pressed or
  minced
2 tablespoons olive oil
½ cup soft bread cubes

¼ cup grated Parmesan
  cheese
½ teaspoon basil leaves
½ teaspoon salt, divided
  Dash black pepper
½ cup shredded mozzarella
  cheese
⅛ teaspoon paprika

Serves 2 to 4

In small bowl or 1-qt. casserole microwave pork sausage at High 2 to 3 minutes, or until meat is no longer pink. Drain. Set aside.

Cut eggplant in half lengthwise. Scoop out pulp, leaving ¼-in. shell. Chop pulp coarsely.

In 2-qt. casserole combine pulp and remaining ingredients except mozzarella and paprika. Cover with wax paper. Microwave at High 6 to 8 minutes, or until vegetables are tender.

Spoon half of stuffing into each eggplant shell. Place stuffed shells in 8 × 8-in. dish. Cover with wax paper. Microwave at High 6 to 7 minutes, or until eggplant is fork tender. Top with mozzarella cheese. Sprinkle with paprika.

Turnip

Kale

Spinach

Collard

Collard

Turnip

Kale

Mustard

Greens

Some greens are delicate in flavor while others taste piquant. Microwave briefly to retain nutrients and character.

How to Select & Store Greens

Choose greens of any type which are clean and crisp. Avoid dry or wilted leaves, seed stems, coarse stems or veins. Spinach should be deep green with either curly or flat leaves. Small yellow leaves are edible, but large ones should be discarded. Select kale, leaf lettuce, and beet, collard, mustard or turnip greens which are green and cold. Avoid woody or flabby stems. Chard should have small dark green leaves and firm, white stalks. Look for lettuce heads which are firm and compact, but not rock hard or heavy.

Place unwashed greens loosely in a plastic bag or covered container to retain humidity. Refrigerate and use promptly. Lettuce will keep a few days and mustard greens a week.

Greens Chart

Type	Amount	Microwave Time at High	Procedure
Fresh Greens			
Beet	1 lb.	7-8½ min.	3-qt. covered casserole with ¼ cup water. Stir once. Let stand 3 to 5 minutes.
Collard, Turnip	2 lbs.	40-45 min.	Wash and cut leaves into 1-in. strips. 3-qt. covered casserole with 2 cups water and 2 slices bacon, cut into fourths. Stir every 5 to 10 minutes.
Kale	1 lb.	14-21 min.	Wash and strip leaves from stems. 3-qt. covered casserole with 1 cup water. Stir every 4 minutes.
Mustard	1 lb.	25-35 min.	Wash and remove stems. 3-qt. covered casserole with 2 cups water and 2 slices bacon, cut into fourths. Stir every 5 to 10 minutes.
Spinach	1 lb.	5-8 min.	Wash and trim. 3-qt. covered casserole. Stir once. Let stand 3 minutes.
Swiss Chard, leaves	1 lb.	5½-6½ min.	Wash and remove stems. Cut leaves into 1-in. strips. 2-qt. covered casserole with ¼ cup water. Stir once. Let stand 3 minutes.
Swiss Chard, stems	1 lb.	7-8 min.	Wash and remove membrane. Cut into 1-in. pieces. 1-qt. covered casserole with ¼ cup water. Let stand 3 minutes.
Frozen Greens			
Collard, Turnip, Kale, chopped	10 oz. pkg.	7-10½ min.	1-qt. covered casserole. Stir once.
Spinach, leaf or chopped	10 oz. pkg.	7-9 min.	1-qt. covered casserole with 2 tablespoons water. Stir once. Let stand 2 to 5 minutes.
Spinach, cut leaf in butter sauce	10 oz. pkg.	5-6½ min.	Flex pouch. Cut large X in one side. Place cut side down in 1-qt. casserole or serving dish. Stir before serving.
Canned Greens			
Kale, Mustard, Turnip, Spinach	15 oz.	2-4 min.	Drain all but 2 tablespoons liquid. 1-qt. covered casserole. Stir once.

Sweet-Sour Spinach ▲

1 lb. fresh spinach
4 slices bacon, cut into eighths
1 tablespoon all-purpose flour
1 tablespoon brown sugar
¼ teaspoon dry mustard
¼ teaspoon salt
    Dash pepper
½ cup half and half
1 tablespoon cider vinegar

Serves 4

Prepare spinach as directed, page 61. Drain; set aside. Microwave bacon in 1½-qt. covered casserole at High 3 to 4 minutes, or until crisp. Drain all but 1 tablespoon fat.

Stir in flour, sugar and seasonings. Blend in half and half. Microwave at High 1 to 1½ minutes, or until thickened; stir once. Stir in vinegar and spinach; toss. Microwave at High 1 to 2 minutes, or until heated.

Lettuce Braised in Stock ▲

¼ cup hot water
1 teaspoon instant chicken
    bouillon granules
4 cups shredded lettuce
1 small carrot, shredded
2 tablespoons chopped onion
2 tablespoons butter or
    margarine
½ teaspoon parsley flakes
⅛ teaspoon salt
    Dash white pepper

Serves 4

In small bowl or 1-cup measure, combine hot water and bouillon. Stir to dissolve.

Combine remaining ingredients in 1½ to 2-qt. casserole. Stir in bouillon. Cover. Microwave at High 2 to 4 minutes, or until lettuce is tender-crisp, stirring after half the cooking time.

Greens With Bacon ▲

4 slices bacon, cut into ¾-in.
    pieces
¼ cup chopped onion
½ teaspoon lemon juice
⅛ teaspoon salt
    Dash nutmeg
    Dash pepper
1 lb. fresh greens (collard,
    mustard or turnip), washed,
    drained and cut into
    1-in. strips

Serves 4

In 3-qt. casserole combine bacon and onion. Cover. Microwave at High 4 to 6 minutes, or until bacon is crisp, stirring after half the time.

Mix in lemon juice and seasonings. Add greens and toss to coat. Cover. Microwave at High 4 to 6 minutes, or until tender-crisp, stirring once.

Spinach & Croutons

2 tablespoons olive or
    vegetable oil
1 small clove garlic, pressed
    or minced
12 oz. fresh spinach, washed
    and well drained
1 teaspoon sesame seeds
3 tablespoons grated
    Parmesan cheese, divided
¼ teaspoon salt
    Dash pepper
2 slices rye or caraway rye
    bread, toasted and cut
    into ½-in. cubes

Serves 4

Preheat 10-in. browning dish at High 3 minutes. In 1-cup measure combine oil and garlic. Add oil mixture to browning dish; tilt to coat dish. Add spinach and sesame seeds. Cover. Microwave at High 1 to 2½ minutes, or just until wilted, stirring after half the time. Drain excess liquid.

Stir in 2 tablespoons cheese, salt and pepper. Sprinkle toast cubes and remaining cheese on top. Serve immediately.

Spinach Soup ►

1 pkg. (10 oz.) frozen
    chopped spinach
¼ cup chopped green onion
2 tablespoons butter or
    margarine
⅓ cup all-purpose flour
1 teaspoon instant chicken
    bouillon granules
½ teaspoon salt
⅛ teaspoon nutmeg
⅛ teaspoon pepper
4 cups milk
2 teaspoons soy sauce
½ cup dairy sour cream

Serves 4

Microwave spinach in package at High 3 to 6 minutes, or until defrosted. Drain well. In 2-qt. casserole place onion and butter. Microwave at High 1½ to 2 minutes, or until tender.

Stir in flour, bouillon and seasonings. Blend in milk and soy sauce. Mix in spinach. Microwave at High 11 to 14 minutes, or until thickened and bubbly, stirring after 5 minutes and then every 2 to 3 minutes. Top servings with sour cream.

Swiss Chard & Mushrooms ►

1 lb. fresh Swiss chard
    or spinach
¼ cup water
1 small onion, chopped
1 tablespoon butter or
    margarine
1 can (7½ oz.) semi-
    condensed savory cream
    of mushroom soup

4 oz. fresh mushrooms, sliced
¼ cup dairy sour cream
½ teaspoon soy sauce
⅛ teaspoon salt
    Dash pepper
    Toasted Almonds,
    page 36

Serves 4

Wash chard; shake off moisture. Cut into 1-in. strips and place in 3-qt. casserole with ¼ cup water. Cover. Microwave at High 5½ to 6½ minutes, or until desired doneness, stirring after half the cooking time. Drain thoroughly.

In 1 to 1½-qt. casserole microwave onion and butter at High 1 to 1½ minutes, or until onion is tender. Add Swiss chard and remaining ingredients except almonds. Blend well.

Microwave at High 1½ to 2 minutes, or until heated through, stirring after half the cooking time. Garnish with toasted almonds.

Jicama

Jicama looks like a turnip and tastes like a water chestnut. The crisp, white, juicy and sweet flesh keeps its texture even when cooked, and absorbs the flavor of dressings or sauces. Serve it raw in salads and with dips, or cooked, as a substitute for potatoes or water chestnuts. Jicama is available in limited supply year-round.

How to Select & Store Jicama

Choose firm, well-shaped roots; smaller ones are best, as large tubers may be woody. Cut off as much as needed. Store in a cool, dry place. After cutting, wrap in foil or plastic, and refrigerate up to a week.

How to Prepare & Microwave Jicama

Peel 1 lb. jicama. Cut into ½-in. cubes or julienne strips, ¼ inch thick and 1½ to 2½ inches long. Place in 2-qt. casserole with ¼ cup water. Cover.

Microwave at High 8 to 9½ minutes, or until jicama is heated, stirring once. Let stand 3 to 5 minutes. Jicama remains tender-crisp.

Serve jicama with ¼ cup honey; butter, salt and pepper; sweet and sour sauce; sour cream; or yogurt dressing.

Jerusalem Artichokes

Jerusalem artichokes, also called sunchokes, are knotty tubers of the sunflower family. They are not artichokes at all, but their flavor is similar to that of artichoke hearts. They have a crisp, crunchy texture and may be served raw in salads or cooked as a potato substitute. Peeling is optional, but the peel will toughen during cooking.

How to Select & Store Jerusalem Artichokes

Choose firm, clean tubers without soft spots. If you plan to peel them, look for the least knobby roots as they will be easier to peel. Refrigerate in sealed plastic bag and use within a week.

How to Prepare & Microwave Jerusalem Artichokes

Scrub 1 lb. chokes under running water. Peel, if desired. Cut into ¼-in. slices. To prevent darkening, place in 1 qt. water with 1 teaspoon lemon juice.

Drain slices. Place in 2-qt. casserole with ¼ cup water and ½ teaspoon lemon juice. Cover. Microwave at High 6 to 9 minutes, or just until fork tender. Do not overcook.

Let stand 3 to 5 minutes. Drain and serve as a vegetable or potato substitute, with butter, salt and pepper; lemon juice and snipped parsley; or Parmesan cheese.

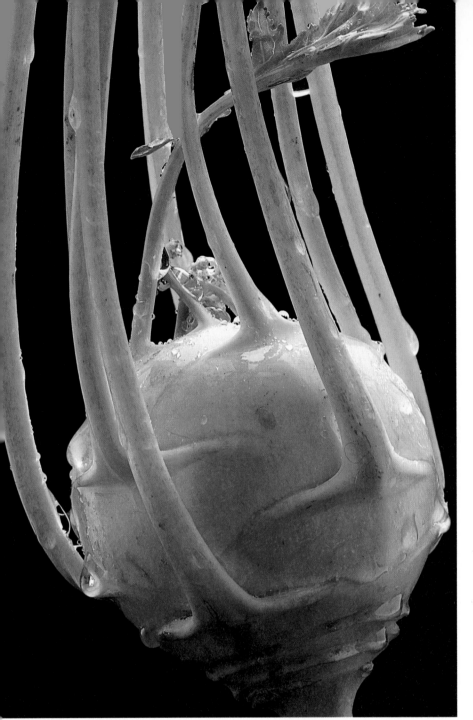

Kohlrabi

Kohlrabi belongs to the cabbage family, but it has a bulbous stem and leaves which resemble a turnip's leaves. The stalk has a crisp texture and mild flavor; young, small kohlrabi leaves may be microwaved like spinach leaves.

How to Select & Store Kohlrabi

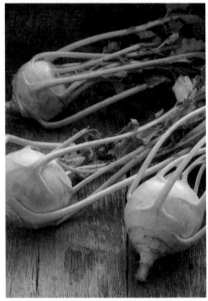

Choose firm, small globes, not more than 3 inches in diameter. Do not wash until ready to cook. Store in plastic bag on the refrigerator shelf and use within a few days. If tops are attached, remove and store in a covered container in the crisper. Use as soon as possible.

How to Prepare & Microwave Kohlrabi

Trim root ends and stems above bulbs from 4 to 5 medium kohlrabi (about 2 lbs.). Scrub and peel bulb. Cut into ¼-in. slices.

Combine in 2-qt. casserole with ¼ cup water; cover. Microwave at High 10 to 15 minutes, or until fork tender, stirring every 4 minutes. Let stand 5 minutes.

Drain and serve with cream sauce and caraway; butter with dill; a dash of Worcestershire; salt and pepper; cheese sauce or sour cream and chives.

Leeks

Leeks are a mild-tasting member of the onion family which resemble large scallions. They are in small supply year-round, with peak seasons spring and fall. Leeks require careful cleaning because they trap dirt as they grow.

How to Select & Store Leeks

Select leeks with fresh, dark green tops and small to medium necks, which are white at least 2 to 3 inches from root end. Straight leeks will be more tender than those with bulbous ends. Slight bruising of tops does not affect quality, but avoid leeks with yellow or wilted tops; they may be old, flabby or tough. Cut off roots and trim tops, leaving 1½ inches of dark green leaves. Remove any dry outer skin. Store in sealed plastic bag on refrigerator shelf and use within a week or two.

How to Prepare & Microwave Leeks

Trim and peel 4 to 5 leeks (1¾ to 2 lbs. untrimmed) as directed above. Pierce leek where white part joins green and pull knife through to top to split the leaves.

Split again at right angles to first. Rinse leeks in cold water to remove dirt. Place in 8 × 8-in. dish with ¼ cup water. Cover with plastic wrap.

Microwave at High 4 to 6½ minutes, or until tender, rotating dish; turn and rearrange leeks. Let stand 3 to 5 minutes. Drain; serve with butter.

Mushrooms

Mushrooms are available all year, with peak supply during the winter months. Mushrooms give off a good deal of liquid when cooked. Use this to enhance the flavor of gravies, sauces or soups. The mushrooms cultivated in the United States are all the same variety, but range in color from white to pale brown. Size helps determine use, not quality. Serve small ones whole, slice the medium-sized and use extra-large for stuffing.

How to Select Mushrooms

Choose firm, clean mushrooms. Those with tightly closed caps are freshest. As mushrooms lose moisture, the 'veil' covering the base of the cap pulls away from the stem.

Gills should be light colored if veils are partially open. Avoid mushrooms with brown or black gills and withered caps which indicate age.

How to Store Mushrooms

Remove tightly sealed plastic wrap from tray or box; re-cover loosely with plastic wrap. Do not wash mushrooms until ready to use. Refrigerate in the crisper for up to 2 or 3 days.

How to Prepare & Microwave Whole Mushrooms

Wash ½ lb. mushrooms gently in cool water, or wipe with damp cloth; do not soak or peel. Pat dry. Cut thin slice off stem. Place in 1-qt. casserole with 2 tablespoons butter.

Do not salt or cover, which darkens the color of fresh mushrooms. Microwave at High, stirring when butter is almost melted, then every 1½ minutes.

Continue microwaving until darkened slightly or mushrooms are tender. Mushrooms of uniform size microwave most evenly. See chart for cooking times.

Mushroom Chart

Type	Amount	Microwave Time at High	Procedure
Fresh Mushrooms Whole	½ lb. (8 oz.)	3-4 min.	Follow photo directions. Let stand 1 to 2 minutes.
	1 lb. (16 oz.)	3½-6½ min.	Follow photo directions. 2-qt. casserole with 3 tablespoons butter. Let stand 1 to 2 minutes.
Slices, ⅛-in.	½ lb. (2-3 cups)	3-6 min.	8 × 8-in. baking dish with 2 tablespoons butter. Cover with plastic wrap. Stir once.

Mushrooms Sautéed ▲ in Sherry

¼ cup chopped green onion
¼ cup sherry
½ teaspoon salt
⅛ teaspoon pepper
16 oz. fresh mushrooms, rinsed
    and drained, halved
 2 tablespoons butter or
    margarine, optional

Serves 4 to 6

In 2-qt. casserole combine onion, sherry, salt and pepper. Add mushrooms; stir to coat. Dot with butter. Cover dish with wax paper. Microwave at High 3 to 7 minutes, or until desired doneness, stirring after half the cooking time.

Serve with steak or hamburgers.

Mushrooms in Garlic Butter

¼ cup butter or margarine
 2 cloves garlic, minced
12 oz. fresh mushrooms, sliced
¼ teaspoon salt
   Dash pepper

Serves 4

Place butter and garlic in 2-qt. casserole. Microwave at High 2½ to 3½ minutes, or until butter melts and garlic browns; stir after half the time.

Add mushrooms, salt and pepper; stir to coat. Cover dish with wax paper. Microwave at High 3 to 5 minutes, or until desired doneness, stirring after half the cooking time.

Serve with steak or hamburgers.

Pickled Mushrooms

12 oz. fresh mushrooms, sliced
 1 medium onion, thinly sliced
 1 green pepper, cut into strips
 1 clove garlic, minced
½ cup wine vinegar
 3 tablespoons olive oil
¼ cup chopped stuffed
    green olives
 1 teaspoon parsley flakes
½ teaspoon salt
¼ teaspoon black pepper
⅛ teaspoon whole thyme
 1 bay leaf

Serves 6

Combine all ingredients in 2-qt. casserole; cover. Microwave at High 5 to 7 minutes, or until vegetables are tender-crisp, stirring after half the time. Refrigerate 6 to 8 hours. Drain.

Layered Casserole

2 cups sliced fresh
    mushrooms
½ cup chopped onion
½ cup chopped celery
2 tablespoons butter or
    margarine
1½ cups crushed seasoned
    bread stuffing mix
¼ cup hot water

4 slices bacon, microwaved
    and crumbled, divided
⅛ teaspoon salt
2 cans (14 oz. each)
    artichoke hearts, drained
    and quartered
3 tablespoons grated
    Parmesan cheese, divided

Serves 4 to 6

In 1½-qt. casserole combine mushrooms, onion, celery and butter.
Cover. Microwave at High 2½ to 4½ minutes, or until tender,
stirring after half the cooking time.

Stir in stuffing mix, hot water, half of bacon and salt. In 1½-qt.
casserole layer half of stuffing, half of artichoke hearts and half of
cheese. Repeat layers. Cover.

Microwave at High 4 to 8 minutes, or until heated through, rotating
dish ½ turn every 3 minutes during cooking. Sprinkle remaining
bacon over top. Microwave, uncovered, at High 1 minute to heat.

Stuffed Mushrooms

8 oz. large fresh mushrooms
¼ cup chopped onion
2 tablespoons butter or
    margarine
¼ cup seasoned bread crumbs
¼ cup shredded cheese (Swiss,
    mozzarella or Cheddar)
2 tablespoons grated
    Parmesan cheese
1 teaspoon parsley flakes
    Dash salt
⅛ teaspoon pepper
¼ teaspoon dry mustard

Serves 4 to 6

Wash mushrooms; remove and
chop stems. In 1-qt. casserole
combine chopped stems, onion
and butter; cover. Microwave at
High 2 minutes, or until tender.
Stir in bread crumbs, cheese
and seasonings. Mound in
mushroom caps.

Arrange caps on paper
towel-lined plate with larger
caps to outside. Microwave at
High 2 to 2½ minutes, or until
heated through, rotating plate
once or twice during cooking.

Mushroom Sauce ►

16 oz. fresh mushrooms,
    sliced ¼ in. thick
1 stalk celery, thinly sliced
⅓ cup chopped green onion
2 tablespoons butter or
    margarine
⅓ cup all-purpose flour
1 teaspoon chervil
½ teaspoon salt
⅛ teaspoon garlic powder
⅛ teaspoon pepper
    Dash cayenne pepper,
    optional
1 bay leaf
½ teaspoon instant chicken
    bouillon granules
1 tablespoon sherry
1½ cups half and half

Serves 4

In 2-qt. casserole combine
vegetables and butter; cover.
Microwave at High 5 to 7
minutes, or until tender, stirring
after half the cooking time.

Mix in flour, seasonings, bouillon
and sherry. Blend in half and
half. Microwave, uncovered, at
High 9 to 10 minutes, or until
thickened and bubbly, stirring
several times.

Serve over spaghetti noodles.

Okra

Okra is especially popular in the South, and a necessary ingredient in Creole gumbos and stews. Inside the okra pod is a sac which releases a gelatineous sap when it is cut or pierced. This liquid thickens gumbos and stews.

How to Select & Store Okra

Select clean, young, white or green pods 2 to 4 inches long. The tip of tender okra bends when pressed and the pod snaps easily. Do not buy dull, dry, shriveled, flabby or discolored pods. Keep okra cool and humid, but not cold. Store uncovered in the crisper; use as soon as possible.

How to Prepare, Microwave & Serve Okra

Wash 1 lb. fresh okra. Trim tip and stem end of pods, being careful not to pierce sac if okra is to be cooked whole.

Slice okra into ½-in. pieces. In 1-qt. casserole combine ¼ cup water, ¼ teaspoon salt and okra; cover. Microwave at High.

Toss whole pods with 2 tablespoons butter or top with Hollandaise Sauce, page 111. For Okra Creole, see page 108.

Okra Chart

Type	Amount	Microwave Time at High	Procedure
Fresh Okra Whole	1 lb.	7-10 min.	Follow photo directions. Let stand, covered, 3 to 5 minutes.
Slices, ½-in.	1 lb. (3 cups)	7-10 min.	Follow photo directions. Let stand, covered, 3 to 5 minutes.
Frozen Okra Whole, slices	10 oz. pkg.	5-7 min.	1-qt. covered casserole with 2 tablespoons water. Stir every 2 minutes.
Canned Okra Cuts	14½ oz.	3-4 min.	2 tablespoons reserved liquid. 1-qt. covered casserole. Stir once or twice.

Onions

Onions are available year-round and are delicious as a vegetable or as flavoring for other dishes. The varieties differ in flavor but can be used interchangeably. Strong smelling onions keep longer than sweet, mild ones. When onions are dried, they develop papery skins which protect them during storage.

Mild Bermuda onions are flat or top shaped, with yellow or white skins and have a short storage life.

Onions of any variety which are 1 to 1½ inches in diameter are identified as boilers (white, right), silverskins or creamers (not pictured). Pearl (small, above) are smaller.

Red Italian onions may be mild to pungent in flavor, depending on growing conditions. They are generally used raw for their color.

Sweet Spanish onions are large, yellow globes with mild flavor. Smaller yellow or white globe onions are more pungent.

Red-brown shallots grow in cloves, like garlic, but have a far milder flavor. Green onion may be any variety which is harvested early and sold fresh.

How to Select Onions

Choose firm, dry onions with papery skins free from green spots and blemishes. Check the necks to avoid fresh sprouts or moisture. Buy green onions with 2 to 3 inches of white stem and crisp green tops.

How to Store Onions

Dry onions keep well up to a month in a cool, dry place. Do not refrigerate or store with potatoes, as onions will absorb moisture and decay more quickly. After cutting, they can be refrigerated several days in a sealed container. Place green onions in plastic bags and refrigerate in the crisper up to a week or two.

How to Microwave Whole Onions

Slice tops from medium onions to expose all layers. Remove root ends and peel. Place onions in baking dish or custard cups. Cover.

Microwave at High for half the cooking time. Rotate each onion in baking dish so side which was next to the outside of the dish is turned toward the center; rotate dish. Custard cups should be rotated and rearranged. Recover; microwave remaining time, or until tender-crisp. Let stand 1 to 2 minutes.

How to Microwave Wedges and Slices

Peel medium onions. Cut each into 8 wedges or ½-in. slices. Place in casserole with 2 tablespoons butter or ¼ cup water.

Reduce cooking odors by microwaving onions uncovered. Cook at High and stir after half the time. When onions are tender-crisp, slightly translucent, and have lost their raw taste, cover and let stand 5 minutes.

74

Stuffed Onions ▶

4 large onions (2½ to 3 lbs.),
    peeled
1 pkg. (10 oz.) frozen green
    peas
4 oz. fresh mushrooms,
    coarsely chopped
¼ teaspoon thyme leaves
⅛ teaspoon pepper
2 tablespoons butter or
    margarine
¼ cup hot water
½ teaspoon instant chicken
    bouillon granules

Serves 4

Hollow out the center of each
onion, leaving ¼-in. thick shell.
(Onion centers may be
chopped and frozen for later
use.) Combine peas, mush-
rooms, thyme and pepper.
Place onion shells in 8 × 8-in.
baking dish and fill each with
one-fourth of the pea and
mushroom stuffing. Dot each
onion with ½ tablespoon butter.

Combine water and bouillon.
Pour over onions. Cover dish
with plastic wrap. Microwave at
High 7 to 10 minutes, or until
tender. Rotate onions once.
Baste with cooking liquid. Let
stand, covered, 3 minutes.

Onion Rings in ▶
Garlic Butter

⅓ cup butter or margarine
2 cloves garlic, pressed or
    minced
¼ teaspoon sugar
⅛ teaspoon white pepper
2 medium onions (1 lb.),
    peeled, thinly sliced and
    separated into rings

Serves 4 to 6

In 2-qt. casserole microwave
butter at High 45 to 60
seconds, or until butter melts.
Stir in garlic, sugar and pepper.
Add onions; toss to coat. Cover;
microwave at High 7 minutes, or
until desired doneness, stirring
after half the cooking time.

French Onion Soup ▲

2 medium-large onions, (1 lb.)
¼ cup butter
2 cans (10½ oz. each) beef
  broth
2½ cups cold water
1 teaspoon sugar
1 tablespoon burgundy wine
⅛ teaspoon pepper

2 tablespoons butter or
  margarine, melted
6 slices French bread
2 tablespoons grated
  Parmesan cheese
6 oz. shredded Gruyère or
  Swiss cheese

Serves 6

Peel onions. Cut in half lengthwise and slice. Set aside. Place butter in 3-qt. casserole. Microwave at High 1 to 1½ minutes, or until melted. Add onion slices, tossing to coat with butter. Cover. Microwave at High 6 to 10 minutes, or until onion is tender, stirring at least twice. Blend in broth, water, sugar, wine and pepper. Cover. Microwave at High 6 to 8 minutes, or until heated.

Brush one side of each slice of French bread with melted butter. Sprinkle with Parmesan cheese. Place under broiler to toast. Ladle soup into 6 individual serving dishes. Top each bowl with toast and 1 oz. shredded Gruyère or Swiss cheese.

Place bowls in oven in circular pattern. Microwave at High 4 to 8 minutes, or until cheese melts and soup is hot.

Glazed Onions ▲

1 lb. pearl onions, peeled
2 tablespoons butter or
  margarine
1 tablespoon brown sugar
½ teaspoon cornstarch
¼ teaspoon salt
¼ teaspoon dry mustard
  Dash pepper
1 tablespoon cider vinegar

Serves 4

In 1 to 1½-qt. casserole combine onions and butter. Cover. Microwave at High 6 to 8 minutes, or until tender, stirring once. Drain; reserve liquid.

In a small bowl combine brown sugar, cornstarch, and seasonings. Stir in vinegar and reserved cooking liquid. Microwave at High 45 to 60 seconds, or until clear and thickened. Pour thickened sauce over onions. Toss to coat.

Scalloped Onions With Cheese ▲

2 medium onions (1 lb.),
   peeled, thinly sliced and
   separated into rings
2 tablespoons water
2 tablespoons butter or
   margarine
2 tablespoons all-purpose
   flour

1 teaspoon parsley flakes
¼ teaspoon salt
¼ teaspoon dry mustard
⅛ teaspoon pepper
1 cup milk
½ cup shredded Cheddar
   cheese

Serves 4

In 2-qt. casserole combine onions and water. Cover. Microwave at High 5 to 7½ minutes, or until tender, stirring after half the cooking time. Set aside.

Place butter in 1-qt. casserole. Microwave at High 45 to 60 seconds, or until melted. Stir in flour and seasonings. Blend in milk. Microwave at High 2½ to 3½ minutes, or until thickened, stirring after 2 minutes and then every minute.

Drain onions. Stir into white sauce. Sprinkle cheese evenly over top. Reduce power to 50% (Medium). Microwave 2 to 4 minutes, or until cheese melts, rotating dish ½ turn after half the time.

Creamed Onions ▲

16 small onions, peeled, or 4
   medium onions, peeled
   and cut into quarters
2 tablespoons water
¾ cup dairy sour cream
¼ cup milk
½ teaspoon salt
   Dash nutmeg
   Dash pepper

Serves 4

In 1½-qt. casserole combine onions and water. Cover. Microwave at High 7 to 8 minutes, or until tender, stirring gently once. Drain.

Combine remaining ingredients. Pour sour cream mixture over onions; toss gently to coat. Reduce power to 50% (Medium). Microwave, uncovered, 1 to 2 minutes, or until sauce is heated through.

Peas

Three types of peas are popular in the United States. The familiar garden or English pea is available January through August, but fresh supplies are limited; most of the crop is frozen or canned. Snow or China peas are edible pods popular in both oriental and French cooking. Peak season is May through September. In the South, black-eyed peas, crowders, purple hulls and field peas are available fresh, frozen, dried or canned. All peas are at their best when young and moist. Unless you grow them yourself, tender peas are hard to find. Those available in markets are more mature. Dried peas are microwaved like dried shell beans, page 29.

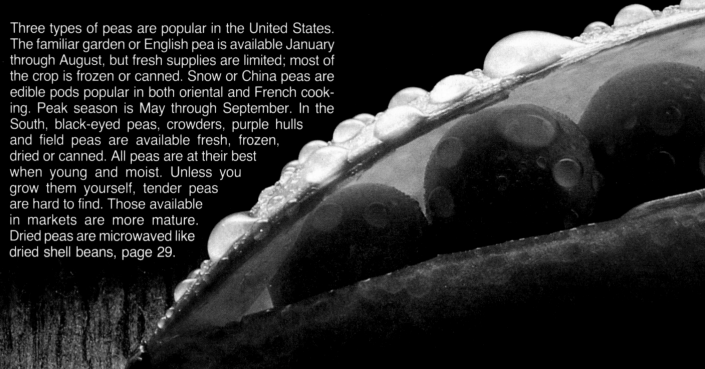

How to Select Peas

Choose garden peas with shiny, bright green pods which are angular, well-filled and crisp enough to snap easily. Light colored, swollen pods indicate over-maturity.

Look for snow, sugar or China pea pods which are flat, firm, crisp and bright green. Select black-eyes with crisp, well filled, unblemished pods.

How to Store Peas

Garden peas must be kept cold from the time they are picked or their sugar turns to starch and they toughen. Refrigerate all peas, unwashed, in plastic bags and use as soon as possible.

How to Prepare & Microwave Garden Peas

Shell 2 lbs. peas just before cooking. Place 2 cups shelled peas in 1½-qt. casserole.

Add 2 tablespoons butter to young peas or ¼ cup water to mature peas. Cover.

Microwave at High until tender, stirring once. See chart, page 80, for cooking times.

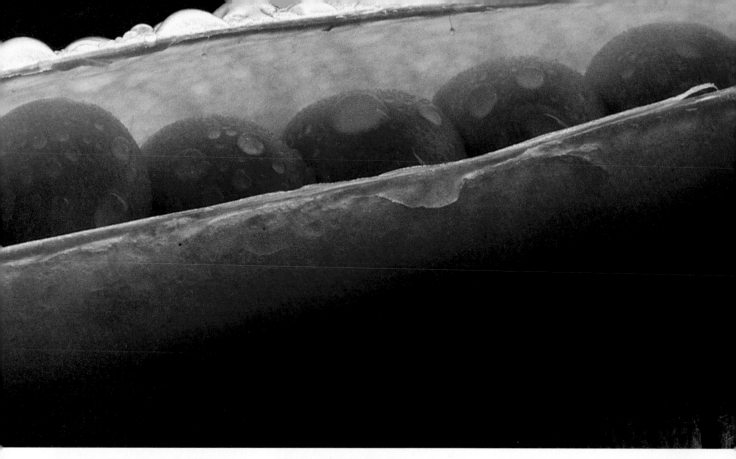

How to Prepare & Microwave Black-eyed Peas

Shell peas just before cooking. Place 2 cups peas in 2-qt. casserole with 1 cup water. Cover with wax paper. A tight cover would cause a boil-over.

Stir peas every 4 minutes during cooking; add more water as needed to keep peas moist and covered.

Microwave at High until peas are as soft as desired and cooking water is slightly thickened. Drain. See chart, page 80, for cooking times.

How to Prepare & Microwave Pea Pods

Cut off end of pod but leave string attached. Pull string down pod. Repeat on other end.

Place pods in 9-in. pie plate with 2 tablespoons water. Cover with plastic wrap.

Microwave until tender-crisp; do not overcook. See chart, page 80 for cooking times.

Peas Chart

Type	Amount	Microwave Time at High	Procedure
Fresh Peas			
Garden Peas	2 lbs. (2 cups)	5-7 min.	Follow photo directions, page 78. Let stand, covered, 3 minutes.
Pea Pods	¼ lb.	2-4 min.	Follow photo directions, page 79. Let stand, covered, 2 minutes.
Black-eyed Peas	2 lbs. (2 cups)	14-18 min.	Follow photo directions, page 79. Let stand, covered, 5 to 10 minutes.
Frozen Peas			
Garden Peas	10 oz. pkg.	4-6 min.	1-qt. covered casserole with 2 tablespoons water. Stir once. Let stand, covered, 3 minutes.
Pea Pods	6 oz. pkg.	3-4 min.	1-qt. covered casserole with 2 tablespoons water. Stir once.
Black-eyed Peas	10 oz. pkg.	8-9 min.	1-qt. covered casserole with ¼ cup water. Stir every 2 minutes. Let stand, covered, 2 minutes.
In butter sauce	10 oz. pkg.	5-6 min.	Flex pouch. Cut large X in one side. Place cut side down in 1-qt. casserole or serving dish. Stir before serving.
Canned Peas			
Garden Peas	16 oz.	2-3 min.	Drain all but 2 tablespoons liquid. 1-qt. covered casserole. Stir once.
Black-eyed Peas	15 oz.	2½-4 min.	Drain all but 2 tablespoons liquid. 1-qt. covered casserole. Stir once.

Peas & Pearl Onions

2 cups fresh shelled or
   1 pkg. (10 oz.) frozen peas
1 cup frozen whole small
   onions
2 tablespoons water
1 tablespoon butter or
   margarine
½ teaspoon chervil
⅛ teaspoon salt
   Dash pepper
1 tablespoon grated
   Parmesan cheese

Serves 4

In 1½-qt. casserole combine peas, onions and water; cover. Microwave at High 5 to 7½ minutes, or until tender, stirring once. Stir in butter, chervil, salt and pepper. Sprinkle with Parmesan before serving.

Minted Peas

2 cups fresh shelled or
   1 pkg. (10 oz.) frozen peas
¼ cup chopped green onion
2 tablespoons butter or
   margarine
1 teaspoon sugar
½ teaspoon dried mint leaves,
   crushed
⅛ teaspoon salt
   Dash whole rosemary,
   crushed
   Dash pepper
½ teaspoon lemon juice

Serves 4

In 1 to 1½-qt. casserole combine all ingredients except lemon juice; cover. Microwave at High 6 minutes, or until tender, stirring once. Stir in lemon juice and serve.

Peas & Mushrooms

2 cups fresh shelled or 1 pkg.
   (10 oz.) frozen peas
4 oz. fresh mushrooms, sliced
   ¼ in. thick
1 to 2 tablespoons butter or
   margarine
⅛ teaspoon salt
⅛ teaspoon marjoram
   Dash pepper

Serves 4

Prepare peas following directions above.

Stir in mushrooms; cover. Microwave at High 1 to 2 minutes, or until mushrooms are tender. Drain. Add remaining ingredients; toss to coat.

Peas With Lettuce ▲

2 cups fresh shelled or 1 pkg.
   (10 oz.) frozen green peas
⅓ cup thinly sliced celery
2 tablespoons water
3 cups shredded head lettuce
1 tablespoon butter or
   margarine, melted
1 tablespoon all-purpose flour
½ teaspoon sugar
¼ teaspoon salt
   Dash pepper
¼ cup whipping cream

Serves 4

In 1½-qt. casserole combine
peas, celery and water; cover.
Microwave at High 5 to 7½
minutes, or until tender. Stir in
lettuce; re-cover. Microwave at
High 1 to 2 minutes, stirring
after every minute. Set aside.

In small dish combine butter,
flour, sugar, salt and pepper.
Blend in cream. Microwave at
High 1 to 2 minutes, or until
thickened, stirring every minute.

Drain vegetables. Add sauce to
vegetables; toss to coat.

Black-eyed Peas & Rice ▶

2 cups fresh shelled or 1 pkg.
   (10 oz.) frozen black-eyed
   peas
2 slices bacon, microwaved
   crisply, crumbled
1 cup water
½ cup chopped green onion
1 clove garlic, pressed or
   minced
1 tablespoon butter or
   margarine
1 can (16 oz.) stewed
   tomatoes
½ cup long grain rice
⅓ cup water
½ teaspoon salt
¼ teaspoon paprika
   Dash cayenne pepper
   Dash black pepper

Serves 4

Prepare black-eyed peas
following directions, page 80.

Stir in remaining ingredients;
cover. Microwave at High 5
minutes. Reduce power to 50%
(Medium). Microwave 20 to 25
minutes, or until rice is tender
and liquid is absorbed, stirring
twice during cooking.

Peppers: Sweet

The familiar green bell pepper turns bright red when fully ripe. Green and red peppers are cooked in the same way, but red have a sweeter taste.

How to Select & Store Peppers

Choose glossy, firm green or red peppers, free from cuts, punctures or soft spots. Relatively heavy weight for the size indicates thick, meaty walls.

Refrigerate peppers in the crisper or cool, humid place. Green peppers keep up to 5 days; use red peppers as soon as possible.

Sautéed Peppers ▶

1 cup green pepper strips, ¼ × 2-in.
1 cup sweet red pepper strips, ¼ × 2-in.
1 cup sliced fresh mushrooms
2 tablespoons olive oil
1 clove garlic, pressed or minced
1 tablespoon chopped pimiento, optional
¼ teaspoon salt
  Dash pepper

Serves 3 to 4

Combine green and red pepper strips and mushrooms in 2-qt. casserole. Add olive oil, garlic, pimiento, salt and pepper. Cover.

Microwave at High 4 to 6 minutes, or until peppers are tender-crisp, stirring once or twice during cooking.

Stuffed Peppers

½ lb. ground beef
½ cup chopped green onion
½ cup chopped celery
1 can (8 oz.) sliced water chestnuts, drained
1¼ cups cooked rice
1 can (7 oz.) cream of mushroom soup
1 teaspoon Worcestershire sauce
¼ teaspoon salt
  Dash garlic powder
  Dash black pepper
2 large peppers, cut in half lengthwise, pulp removed
  Paprika, optional

Serves 4

In 1½-qt. casserole combine ground beef, onion, celery and water chestnuts. Microwave at High 4 minutes, or until meat is no longer pink, stirring to break up after half the cooking time. Drain. Stir in rice, soup, Worcestershire sauce, salt, garlic powder and black pepper. Spoon mixture evenly into pepper halves.

Place peppers filled side up on microwave roasting rack. Cover with wax paper. Microwave at High 5 minutes. Rearrange peppers. Reduce power to 50% (Medium). Microwave 12 to 15 minutes, or until filling is hot and peppers are tender, rearranging after half the cooking time. If desired, sprinkle with paprika before serving.

Potatoes

In general, russets produce a drier and fluffier baked potato, while the firm, moist red and white potatoes keep their shape better in salads, stews or soups. Mature potatoes are available all year. New potatoes, with waxy flesh and tender skins, are freshly dug potatoes of any variety. Serve them steamed or creamed. They are marketed in late winter or early spring.

How to Store Potatoes

Store potatoes unwashed and unwrapped at room temperature or slightly cooler in a dark, well-ventilated area. Do not refrigerate. At temperatures below 50°, the starch in potatoes converts to sugar, producing undesirable flavor. Properly stored, they keep well for several weeks.

How to Select Potatoes

Choose firm, smooth, clean and reasonably well shaped potatoes to minimize preparation waste. Avoid irregularly shaped, knobby potatoes, and those with large cuts, cracks, skinned areas, black spots, sprouting eyes. Green areas should be cut out before cooking.

How to Microwave Baked Potatoes

Prick well-scrubbed medium potatoes. Arrange on paper towel at least 1 inch apart.

Turn potatoes over and rearrange after half the time. See chart for cooking times.

Wrap potatoes in foil or cover with casserole to hold in heat. Let stand 5 to 10 minutes.

How to Microwave "Boiling" Potatoes

Scrub but do not peel whole new potatoes. Prick twice with fork. Place in 1½ to 2-qt. casserole with 2 tablespoons water; cover.

Peel red or white potatoes. Cut in quarters, ¼-in. thick slices, or cubes. Combine ¼ cup water and ½ teaspoon salt. Mix with potatoes in casserole; cover.

Microwave at High until fork tender; stir or rearrange new potatoes from center to outside of dish after half the time. See chart for cooking times.

Potato Chart

Type	Amount	Microwave Time at High	Procedure
Fresh Potatoes			
Baked	1 med.	3-5 min.	Follow photo directions, page 85. Let stand 5 to 10 minutes.
	2 med.	5-7½ min.	
	3 med.	7-10 min.	
	4 med.	10½-12½ min.	
Boiled			
Whole, new	8	5-8 min.	Follow photo directions, page 85. Let stand 3 minutes.
	12	8-10 min.	
Slices, ¼-in.	4 med.	8-10 min.	Follow photo directions, page 85. Let stand 3 minutes.
	6 med.	9-11 min.	
Cubes, 1-in.	4 med.	7-8 min.	Follow photo directions, page 85. Let stand 3 minutes.
	6 med.	8-12 min.	
Quarters	4 med.	7-9 min.	Follow photo directions, page 85. Let stand 3 minutes.
	6 med.	9-11 min.	

German Potato Salad

4 medium red potatoes, peeled and cubed
¼ cup chopped onion
3 slices bacon, cut into eighths
1 tablespoon all-purpose flour
¼ cup cider vinegar
2 tablespoons sugar
½ teaspoon celery seed
½ teaspoon salt
Dash pepper

Serves 4 to 6

Prepare potatoes as directed, page 85.

Place onion and bacon in 1½ to 2-qt. casserole. Microwave at High 3 to 4 minutes, or until onion is tender and bacon is lightly browned, stirring once during cooking time. Blend in flour. Add cooked potatoes and remaining ingredients, stirring to combine. Microwave at High 3 to 4 minutes, or until mixture is slightly thickened, stirring after half the cooking time.

Scalloped Potatoes

¼ cup butter or margarine
3 tablespoons all-purpose flour
2 teaspoons chopped chives, divided
1 teaspoon salt
½ teaspoon dry mustard
⅛ teaspoon pepper
1¾ cups milk
4 medium potatoes, sliced

Serves 4 to 6

Microwave butter in 2-qt. casserole at High 45 seconds to 1¼ minutes, or until melted. Stir in flour, chives, salt, dry mustard and pepper. Blend in milk. Microwave at High 5 to 7 minutes, or until thickened, stirring every other minute.

Mix in potatoes. Cover. Microwave at High 15 to 20 minutes, or until potatoes are tender, stirring 2 or 3 times.

Variation:
Scalloped Potatoes Au Gratin:
Add ¾ to 1 cup grated cheese to sauce. Stir until melted.

Chunky Potato Soup

4 slices bacon, cut into eighths
3 medium potatoes, peeled and cut into ½-in. cubes
2 stalks celery, chopped
1 medium onion, chopped
¼ cup water
⅛ teaspoon pepper
2½ cups milk, divided
¼ cup all-purpose flour
1 teaspoon salt

Makes 1 quart

Microwave bacon in covered 2-qt. casserole at High 5 to 6 minutes, or until lightly browned. Bacon will not be crisp. Drain.

Add potatoes, celery, onion, water and pepper. Cover. Microwave at High 10 to 12 minutes, or until vegetables are tender, stirring once.

Combine ½ cup milk with flour until smooth. Stir flour mixture, salt and remaining milk into potatoes. Microwave, uncovered, at High 7 to 10 minutes, or until thickened, stirring twice during cooking time.

Spanish Potatoes ▲

2 large potatoes, peeled, if
    desired and sliced
    ⅛ to ½ in. thick
1 small clove garlic, pressed or
    minced
2 tablespoons olive oil
4 oz. fresh mushrooms, sliced
1 small onion, thinly sliced and
    separated into rings
½ teaspoon salt
    Dash pepper

Serves 4

In 2-qt. casserole combine
potatoes, garlic and olive oil;
cover. Microwave at High 6
minutes, stirring after half the
cooking time.

Add remaining ingredients.
Cover; microwave at High 4 to 8
minutes, or until vegetables are
tender, stirring after half the
cooking time.

Stuffed Potatoes ▲

4 medium potatoes, scrubbed
½ cup dairy sour cream
⅓ cup milk
2 tablespoons grated
    Parmesan cheese
¾ teaspoon salt
⅛ teaspoon pepper
1 teaspoon chopped chives
    or parsley flakes
2 tablespoons sliced almonds,
    optional
⅛ teaspoon paprika

Serves 4

Prick potatoes twice with a fork. Arrange potatoes at least 1 inch
apart on paper towel placed on oven floor. Microwave at High 10½
to 12½ minutes, or until still slightly firm, rearranging and turning
over after half the cooking time. Cover with an inverted casserole
and let stand 5 to 10 minutes.

Slice top from each potato; scoop out center. Mash with sour
cream, milk, cheese, salt, pepper and chives. Spoon into shells.*

Sprinkle with almonds and paprika. Place on serving plate or on
paper towel in oven. Microwave at High 2 to 4 minutes, or until
thoroughly heated, rotating plate ½ turn or rearranging after half
the cooking time.

*Can be prepared to this step the night before. Refrigerate. Add ½
minute per potato to reheat time.

Rutabagas

Turnips

Parsnips

Rutabagas, Turnips & Parsnips

Rutabagas, turnips and parsnips are plentiful from late fall to spring. Turnips are similar to potatoes in texture, but stronger in flavor. Rutabagas are sweeter than turnips; parsnips have a sweet, nutty flavor.

Stem and peel roots just before cooking. Cut rutabagas into ½-in. cubes. Turnips may be cubed or sliced. Slice or halve young parsnips, then cut into 2-in. lengths. Quarter large parsnips and remove the woody core.

Serve roots with butter, salt and pepper. Parsnips may be topped with sour cream and chives. To prepare mashed roots, cook them a little longer, or until soft. Purée them with their cooking liquid and butter, adding more water if needed.

How to Select & Store Rutabagas, Turnips & Parsnips

Choose roots which are firm, smooth and clean. Rutabagas should be heavy for their size, and are usually waxed to retain moisture. Small to medium sized turnips and parsnips are best; large ones may be woody. Place roots in a sealed plastic bag and refrigerate. They keep well for long periods of time.

Rutabagas, Turnips & Parsnips Chart

Type	Amount	Microwave Time at High	Procedure
Fresh Rutabagas Cubes, ½-in.	1½ lbs. (3-4 cups)	14-18 min.	2-qt. covered casserole with ¼ cup water. Stir every 3 minutes. Let stand, covered, 3 minutes.
Fresh Turnips Slices, ¼-in.	4 med. (1½ lbs.)	9-11 min.	1-qt. covered casserole with ¼ cup water. Stir once. Let stand, covered, 3 minutes.
Cubes, ½-in.	4 med. (1½ lbs.)	12-14 min.	1-qt. covered casserole with ¼ cup water. Stir once. Let stand, covered, 2 minutes.
Fresh Parsnips Slices, Cuts, Quarters	4 med. (1 lb.)	5-7 min.	1-qt. covered casserole with ¼ cup water. Stir once. Let stand, covered, 3 minutes.
Canned Rutabagas Diced	16½ oz.	2-4 min.	Drain all but 2 tablespoons liquid. 1-qt. covered casserole. Stir once.

Rutabaga Casserole

3 cups pared, cubed rutabaga
¼ cup water
¼ teaspoon salt, divided
1 large apple, peeled, chopped
2 tablespoons butter or
  margarine
¼ cup brown sugar
  Dash nutmeg
  Dash pepper
2 tablespoons chopped pecans

Serves 4

In 1½-qt. casserole combine rutabaga, water and ⅛ teaspoon salt; cover. Microwave at High 7 to 11 minutes, or until fork tender, stirring once. Set aside.

In small dish microwave apple and butter at High 1 to 2 minutes, or until almost tender, stirring once. Set aside.

Drain rutabaga. Add apple and butter mixture, brown sugar, remaining salt, nutmeg and pepper, stirring until sugar melts. Mix in chopped pecans; serve immediately.

Variation:
Substitute cubed turnip for half of rutabaga.

Parsnips With Pineapple ▶

4 medium or 1 lb. parsnips,
  pared and cut into julienne
  strips
2 tablespoons butter or
  margarine
½ cup water, divided
2 tablespoons brown sugar
1½ teaspoons cornstarch
1 can (8 oz.) crushed
  pineapple
1 teaspoon grated orange rind
⅛ teaspoon salt

Serves 4

In 1½ to 2-qt. casserole combine parsnips, butter and ¼ cup of the water. Cover; microwave at High 5 to 7 minutes, or until tender-crisp. Set aside.

In 1-qt. measure or casserole combine brown sugar and cornstarch. Stir in remaining water, the pineapple, grated orange rind and salt. Microwave at High 3 to 4 minutes, or until thickened, stirring after 2 minutes and then every minute.

Drain parsnips; pour pineapple mixture over.

89

Yellow
Straightneck

Hubbard

Zucchini

Butternut

Butternut

Spaghetti Squash

Acorn

Buttercup

Yellow
Crookneck

Squash

The traditional terms, "summer" and "winter" squash refer to type and use, rather than seasonal availability; some variety of either type is in the market year-round.

"Summer" varieties are tender, immature, very moist squashes with edible seeds and rind. Small ones are best, although you can use more mature ones if you peel them and scoop out the seeds before cooking.

"Winter" squashes are picked when they are mature and have developed hard rinds. The tough seeds and fibrous center are inedible and must be scooped out.

Refrigerate summer squash in plastic bags and use within a few days. Whole winter squash will keep 3 to 6 months in a cool, dry, well-ventilated place. Hanging them in net bags is ideal. Cover cut pieces with plastic wrap and refrigerate in the crisper. Use as soon as possible; chilling converts their starch to sugar, producing undesirable flavors.

How to Select Summer Squash

Look for pattypans or scallops 3 to 4 inches in diameter; zucchini and cocozelle under 8 inches and yellow straightnecks or crooknecks from 4 to 6 inches long. Avoid large squashes, or those with dull appearance and hard, tough rind.

Choose small to medium squashes which are firm, heavy for their size, have very tender rinds and soft seeds.

How to Select Winter Squash

Buy whole squashes which feel hard, and have no soft spots or cracks. A squash which is heavy for its size will have a thick wall of edible flesh. Tender shells indicate immaturity and poor eating and keeping qualities. Pictured left to right: acorn, butternut, buttercup and Mediterranean.

Unusual winter squashes are spaghetti, named for the long, thin strands of flesh, and chayote, which has one large seed and a thin rind which should be peeled.

How to Microwave Acorn Squash

Wash 1½-lb. squash and halve lengthwise. If squash is hard to cut, microwave 1 to 2 minutes at High. Scoop out seeds and fibers.

Cover each squash half with plastic wrap. Arrange in oven with space between.

Microwave at High until tender, rotating and rearranging after half the time. See chart for cooking and standing times.

How to Microwave Buttercup, Butternut, Banana or Hubbard Squash

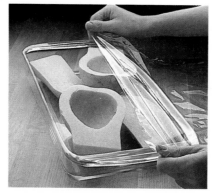

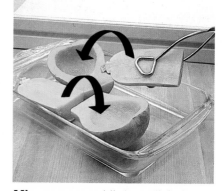

Wash squash and cut in ½-lb. pieces. Scoop out seeds and fibers. When cooking 1 or 2 pieces, wrap each piece in plastic wrap.

Arrange 4 pieces in 8 × 8 or 12 × 8-in. baking dish. Cover with plastic wrap.

Microwave at High until fork tender, rearranging 2 or more pieces after half the cooking time. See chart for cooking times. Serve in shell with butter and pecans or walnuts.

How to Microwave Spaghetti Squash

Wash squash. Pierce rind deeply several times with sharp knife for steam outlets. Place on paper towel in oven.

Microwave at High until squash yields to pressure and feels soft. See chart for cooking times.

Halve crosswise. Scoop out seeds and fibers. Twist out long strands of flesh with fork.

How to Microwave Zucchini, Cocozelle or Yellow Squash

Wash 10-oz. squash gently but well to remove any grit. Trim ends and slice ¼ inch thick.

Place in shallow 2-qt. casserole with 2 tablespoons butter for flavor. Cover.

Microwave at High until desired tenderness, stirring after half the time. See chart for cooking times.

Squash Chart

Type	Amount	Microwave Time at High	Procedure
Fresh Winter Squash			
Acorn, whole (1½-lb.)	½ squash 1 squash 2 squash	5-8 min. 8½-11½ min. 13-16 min.	Follow photo directions opposite. Let stand, covered, 5 to 10 minutes.
Buttercup, Butternut, Banana, Hubbard, Mediterranean, pieces (½-lb.)	1 piece 2 pieces 4 pieces	3-4½ min. 4-6½ min. 5½-12 min.	Follow photo directions. Let stand, covered, 5 minutes.
Patty Pan, mature, whole (½-lb.)	1 squash 2 squash	2-4¼ min.	Cut off tops. Remove seeds. Cover with plastic wrap. Let stand, covered, 3 minutes.
Fresh Summer Squash			
Zucchini, slices (¼-in.)	2 cups	2½-6½ min.	Follow photo directions. Let stand, covered, 2 minutes.
Yellow, slices (¼-in.)	2 cups	4½-7½ min.	Follow photo directions. Let stand, covered, 2 to 3 minutes.
Spaghetti, whole	1 lb.	4-6½ min.	Follow photo directions. Let stand, covered, 5 minutes.
Patty Pan, immature, cubes (¾-in.)	4 cups	9-11 min.	1½-qt. covered casserole with 2 tablespoons water. Stir twice.
Frozen Squash			
Mashed	12 oz. pkg.	5½-8 min.	1-qt. covered casserole. Break apart after 2 minutes; stir at 2 minute intervals.
Zucchini, slices	10 oz. pkg.	4½-6½ min.	1-qt. covered casserole. Stir once. Let stand, covered, 2 minutes.
Canned Squash			
Yellow, Zucchini	16 oz.	2-4 min.	Drain all but 2 tablespoons liquid. 1-qt. covered casserole. Stir once.

Parmesan Squash Ring ▼

½ cup chopped green onion
2 tablespoons butter or
    margarine
2 pkgs. (12 oz. each) frozen
    squash, defrosted, or
    4 cups fresh, cooked
    and mashed
½ teaspoon salt
¼ teaspoon red pepper
1 cup grated Parmesan cheese
4 eggs

Serves 6 to 8

Place onion and butter in
medium bowl. Microwave at
High 1 to 1½ minutes, or until
onion is tender. Stir in remaining
ingredients. Pour into greased
9-in. ring mold. Microwave at
High 13 to 18½ minutes, or until
set, rotating ¼ turn every 3
minutes. Let stand 8 minutes.
Loosen edges and invert onto
serving dish.

Stuffed Acorn Squash

2 medium acorn squash,
    halved

Filling:
2 medium apples, peeled, if
    desired, cored and
    chopped
2 tablespoons water

Topping:
3 tablespoons brown sugar

3 tablespoons chopped
    pecans
1 tablespoon butter or
    margarine
1 teaspoon all-purpose
    flour
¼ teaspoon cinnamon

Serves 4

Scoop out seeds from squash halves. Place cut-side down on
microwave baking sheet or in 12 × 8-in. baking dish. Cover with
plastic wrap. Microwave at High 8 to 12 minutes, or until fork
tender, rotating dish ½ turn after half the cooking time. Let stand
while preparing filling.

In 1-qt. casserole combine apples and water. Cover. Microwave at
High 4 to 6 minutes, or until tender, stirring after half the cooking
time. Set aside.

Combine topping ingredients in small bowl until crumbly.

Turn squash cut-side up. Place one-fourth of apples in each half.
Sprinkle one-fourth of topping on each. Cover with wax paper.
Microwave at High 2½ to 3 minutes, or until topping melts, rotating
dish ½ turn after half the cooking time.

Pumpkin Bars ▲

1 cup all-purpose flour
¾ cup brown sugar
1 cup cooked or canned
    pumpkin
½ teaspoon baking powder
½ teaspoon baking soda
¼ teaspoon salt

1 teaspoon pumpkin pie
    spice
⅓ cup chopped nuts
¼ cup raisins
1 egg
    Cream Cheese Frosting,
    page 47

Makes 8 × 8-in. dish

Place all ingredients except frosting in mixing bowl. Blend at low speed; then beat at medium speed 1 minute. Spread batter in 8 × 8-in. baking dish.

Place dish on inverted saucer. Microwave at 50% (Medium) 6 minutes, rotating ¼ turn every 1 to 2 minutes. Increase power to High. Microwave 5 to 6 minutes, rotating ¼ turn every 2 minutes, until very little unbaked batter appears through bottom of dish. Let stand 5 to 10 minutes. Cool before frosting.

Seasoned Patty Pan

4 cups cubed patty pan
    squash, ¾-in. (about 1 lb.)
1 tablespoon butter or
    margarine
1 tablespoon water*
1 teaspoon chopped chives
½ teaspoon salt
⅛ teaspoon garlic powder
    Dash nutmeg
    Dash pepper

Serves 4

In 1½-qt. casserole combine all ingredients. Cover. Microwave at High 6 to 12 minutes, or until squash is translucent, stirring twice during cooking.

*Or omit water and use 2 tablespoons butter.

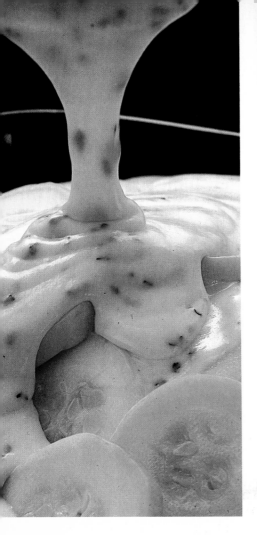

Squash in Cream Sauce ▲

1 lb. yellow summer squash,
   cut into ¼-in. slices
2 tablespoons water
1 tablespoon butter or
   margarine
1 tablespoon all-purpose flour
½ teaspoon chervil
½ teaspoon salt
   Dash pepper
¼ teaspoon sugar
½ cup half and half

Serves 4 to 6

In 1½-qt. casserole combine
squash and water. Cover.
Microwave at High 5 to 7
minutes, or until fork tender; stir
once. Drain and set aside.

In small bowl melt butter at
High 15 to 30 seconds. Stir in
flour, seasonings and sugar.
Blend in half and half. Microwave at High 1½ to 2½ minutes, or until thickened, stirring
twice. Pour sauce over squash
and toss to coat.

Stuffed Zucchini ▲

2 medium zucchini
1 small onion, chopped
1 cup coarsely chopped fresh
   mushrooms
½ cup chopped celery
1 medium tomato, chopped
1 tablespoon butter or
   margarine

¾ cup soda cracker crumbs
1 egg
½ cup grated Cheddar cheese
2 tablespoons grated
   Parmesan cheese
½ teaspoon salt
⅛ teaspoon pepper
½ teaspoon paprika

Serves 4

Halve zucchini lengthwise. Scoop out pulp leaving ¼-in. shell;
chop pulp coarsely. Combine with onion, mushrooms, celery
and tomatoes in 1½ to 2-qt. casserole. Cover. Microwave at
High 4 to 6 minutes, or until tender, stirring once during cooking
time. Drain.

Stir in cracker crumbs, egg, Cheddar cheese, Parmesan
cheese, salt and pepper. Mound one-fourth of filling in each
zucchini shell. Sprinkle with paprika.

Arrange stuffed zucchini on microwave roasting rack. Cover with
plastic wrap. Microwave at High 5 to 7 minutes, or until filling is
set and zucchini is fork tender, rotating dish ½ turn and
rearranging zucchini after half the cooking time.

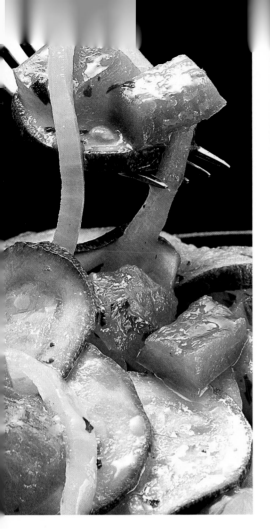

Italian Zucchini ▲

2 cups thinly sliced zucchini
1 medium onion, thinly sliced
1 clove garlic, pressed or
  minced
½ medium green pepper,
  chopped
1 tablespoon olive oil
½ teaspoon basil leaves
½ teaspoon salt
  Dash pepper
1 medium tomato, peeled if
  desired, cut into ½-in.
  chunks

Serves 4

Combine all ingredients except
tomatoes in 2-qt. casserole.
Cover. Microwave at High 4 to
5 minutes, or until zucchini is
tender-crisp. Stir in tomatoes.
Re-cover; microwave at High 1
to 2½ minutes, or until
tomatoes are tender.

Zucchini Bread ▲

1 cup all-purpose flour
1 teaspoon baking powder
1 teaspoon baking soda
  Pinch salt
1½ teaspoons cinnamon
½ cup vegetable oil
2 eggs

1½ cups shredded, unpeeled
  zucchini
1 teaspoon vanilla
2 tablespoons molasses
⅔ cup sugar
2 tablespoons wheat germ,
  optional

Makes 9x5-in. loaf

Blend all ingredients in mixing bowl at low speed until
moistened; beat at medium speed 1 minute.

Spread batter in 9x5-in. loaf dish lined on bottom with wax
paper. If desired, sprinkle loaf with wheat germ. Shield ends of
loaf with 2-in. wide strips of foil, covering 1 inch of batter and
molding remainder around handles.

Center loaf dish on inverted saucer in oven. Microwave at 50%
(Medium) 6 minutes, rotating ¼ turn every 1 to 2 minutes.
Increase power to High. Microwave 1 to 4 minutes, rotating ¼
turn every 1 to 2 minutes. If using clear glass dish, check for
doneness by looking through bottom. No unbaked batter should
appear in center. Let stand directly on countertop 5 to 10
minutes before removing from dish.

Sweet Potatoes & Yams

Sweet potatoes are of two types. Dry-meated sweet potatoes have light tan skin and pale flesh which is similar to a white potato in texture. Moist-meated sweet potatoes, often called "yams" in Southern regions of the country, have tan to red-brown skin and sweet orange flesh. Use interchangeably. For best nutrition, microwave in the jackets and slip the skins off after cooking. Follow the time chart below and the technique for baked potatoes, page 86. Sweet potatoes are plentiful from October through April, with the yam type in greatest supply.

How to Select & Store Sweet Potatoes

Choose chunky medium-sized sweet potatoes or yams which are firm, smooth and tapered at the ends. Avoid decayed spots; even when cut away, they affect the flavor of the remaining flesh. Keep sweet potatoes in a cool, dry, well-ventilated place. Do not refrigerate. Use within a few weeks; sweets do not keep as well as white potatoes.

Sweet Potato Pie Pictured opposite

2 eggs
1½ cups cooked, mashed
    sweet potatoes
⅔ cup brown sugar
1¼ cups evaporated milk
1 tablespoon all-purpose flour
1 teaspoon cinnamon
½ teaspoon nutmeg
¼ teaspoon ginger
⅛ teaspoon ground cloves
⅛ teaspoon salt
1 microwaved 9-in. pie
    shell, page 118

Makes one 9-in. pie

Blend all filling ingredients at low speed in a medium bowl. Microwave at High 3 minutes, stirring once. Reduce power to 50% (Medium). Microwave 7 to 8 minutes, or until very hot and slightly thickened, stirring with whisk every 2 minutes.

Pour into prepared shell. Microwave on wax paper at 50% (Medium) 10 to 13 minutes, or until set in center, rotating ¼ turn every 3 minutes. Cool. Serve with whipped cream or ice cream.

Sweet Potato Casserole

4 medium yams, cooked
    and peeled or 1½ lbs.
    canned yams, drained
¼ cup half and half
2 tablespoons butter
    or margarine
1 cup dairy sour cream, divided
1 egg
2 tablespoons brown sugar
½ teaspoon cinnamon
¼ teaspoon nutmeg
¼ teaspoon salt
    Dash pepper
2 tablespoons chopped walnuts

Serves 4 to 6

In medium bowl whip yams, half and half and butter until smooth. Blend in ¾ cup sour cream, egg, brown sugar, and spices. Spoon into 1-qt. casserole. Cover with wax paper.

Microwave at High 1½ minutes. Reduce power to 50% (Medium). Microwave 6 to 8 minutes, or until almost set, rotating dish ¼ turn 2 or 3 times. Spread with remaining sour cream. Sprinkle with walnuts. Microwave at 50% (Medium) 2 to 4 minutes, or until topping is heated, rotating dish ½ turn once.

Sweet Potato and Yam Chart

Type	Amount	Microwave Time at High	Procedure
Fresh Sweet Potatoes and Yams Whole (5-7 oz. each)	1 potato 2 potatoes 3 potatoes 4 potatoes	3-5 min. 5-9 min. 6½-10 min. 8-13 min.	Wash and prick with fork. Place in oven on paper towel. Rearrange once. Let stand 3 minutes.

Tomatoes

Tomatoes are available year round, but the best time to enjoy them is when home-grown varieties are on the market. For peak flavor, tomatoes should be picked when nearly ripe, and kept at room temperature. A ripe tomato is delicate and highly perishable, so shipped-in tomatoes are picked when they are fully developed but still pink or partially green. (This stage is called "vine-ripe.") If not chilled, they will develop red color, but not full flavor. Once chilled, tomatoes will not ripen further.

How to Select & Store Tomatoes

Choose plump tomatoes that are heavy for their size, firm to slightly soft, and well-formed for their variety. Regular and cherry tomatoes are round. Pear-shaped plum or Roma tomatoes are meatiest and best for sauces. Tomatoes need not be fully red, but should be free from bruises, brown spots, scars or cracks. Over-ripe tomatoes are very soft with watery, depressed areas.

Refrigerate fully ripe tomatoes if necessary and use within 3 days. Under-ripe tomatoes which have not been chilled will ripen at room temperature away from direct sunlight.

Italian Sauce ▶

1 lb. ground beef
¼ lb. ground pork sausage
1 medium onion, chopped
1 stalk celery, thinly sliced
2 cloves garlic, pressed
   or minced
½ medium green pepper,
   chopped
8 medium Roma tomatoes,
   cut into 1-in. cubes
1 can (8 oz.) tomato sauce

1 can (6 oz.) tomato paste
¼ cup red wine, beef broth
   or water
1 teaspoon salt
1 teaspoon basil
1 teaspoon oregano leaves
⅛ teaspoon black pepper
1 bay leaf
1 teaspoon marjoram
1 teaspoon sugar

Makes 2 quarts

In 2 to 3-qt. casserole combine ground beef, sausage, onion, celery, garlic and green pepper. Cover. Microwave at High 5 to 7 minutes, or until meat is no longer pink, stirring to break up meat after half the time. Drain.

Stir in remaining ingredients. Cover. Microwave at High 5 minutes. Stir. Reduce power to 50% (Medium). Microwave uncovered 20 to 25 minutes, or until desired consistency, stirring 2 or 3 times.

Variation: Substitute 1 can (16 oz.) whole tomatoes for fresh.

101

◀ Hot Vinaigrette Tomatoes

½ cup olive or salad oil
3 tablespoons wine vinegar
2 tablespoons chopped
   green pepper
1 tablespoon sweet pickle
   relish
1 clove garlic, pressed or
   minced

1 teaspoon chopped chives
½ teaspoon oregano
¼ teaspoon salt
⅛ teaspoon pepper
4 medium ripe tomatoes,
   sliced ½ in. thick
¼ cup chopped green onion

Serves 4

Combine all ingredients except tomatoes and green onion in shallow dish or casserole. Add tomato slices, turning to coat with marinade. Let stand at room temperature 2 to 2½ hours.

Remove tomato slices from marinade and place in single layer in 8 × 12-in. dish. Sprinkle with green onion. Spoon 2 tablespoons marinade over top. Cover dish with plastic wrap. Microwave at High 3 to 5 minutes, or until tomatoes are heated through, rotating dish ½ turn after half the cooking time.

Cream of Tomato Soup

4 medium ripe tomatoes, cut
   into 1-in. chunks
¼ cup chopped onion
2 teaspoons sugar
1 bay leaf
2 tablespoons butter or
   margarine

2 tablespoons all-purpose
   flour
½ teaspoon salt
⅛ teaspoon pepper
⅛ teaspoon celery seed
1⅓ cups milk

Serves 2

In 1½ to 2-qt. casserole combine tomatoes, onion, sugar and bay leaf. Cover. Microwave at High 7 to 10 minutes, or until tomatoes soften and flavors blend, stirring once or twice during cooking. Sieve mixture (about 1 to 1½ cups) and set aside.

In 1 to 1½-qt. casserole melt butter at High 30 to 45 seconds. Stir in flour and seasonings. Blend in milk. Microwave at High 4 to 5 minutes, or until thickened and bubbly, stirring after 2 minutes and then every minute.

Slowly add tomato mixture to thickened sauce, stirring constantly. Serve immediately. Top individual servings with croutons or crisp, crumbled bacon, if desired.

Variation:
Substitute 1 can (16 oz.) whole tomatoes, drained and ⅓ cup liquid reserved, for fresh. Combine tomatoes, reserved liquid, onion, sugar and bay leaf. Cover. Microwave at High 5 to 6 minutes, stirring once or twice during cooking. Sieve mixture (about 1 to 1½ cups) and proceed as above.

Stuffed Tomatoes ►

4 medium ripe tomatoes
4 slices bacon, cut into ½-in.
    wide strips
2 tablespoons finely
    chopped onion
2 tablespoons finely
    chopped celery
1 cup cooked, drained peas

¼ cup crushed dry bread
    crumbs
1 tablespoon hot water
1 tablespoon grated
    Parmesan cheese
1 teaspoon parsley flakes
⅛ teaspoon thyme leaves
    Dash pepper

Serves 4

Remove stem ends of tomatoes and scoop out center
pulp and seeds. Place tomatoes in 8 × 8-in. baking dish; set aside.

In 1-qt. casserole combine bacon pieces, onion and celery. Cover.
Microwave at High 3 to 4 minutes, or until vegetables are tender.
Stir in peas, bread crumbs, water, cheese and seasonings.

Spoon stuffing into tomatoes. Cover dish with plastic wrap.
Microwave at High 2½ to 3½ minutes, or until tomatoes are heated
through, rotating dish ½ turn after half the time.

Scalloped Tomatoes

4 slices bacon
½ cup chopped celery
⅓ cup chopped onion
2 tablespoons butter or
    margarine
2½ tablespoons all-purpose
    flour
4 medium ripe tomatoes,
    peeled* and cut
    into ½-in. cubes

1 cup dry bread cubes,
1½ teaspoons sugar
½ teaspoon salt
¼ teaspoon dry mustard
⅛ teaspoon pepper

Serves 4

Place bacon strips between double thickness of paper towels.
Microwave at High 3 to 4 minutes, or until crisp. Set aside to cool.

In 1 to 1½-qt. casserole combine celery, onion and butter. Cover.
Microwave at High 2 to 4 minutes, or until tender. Stir in flour. Add
tomatoes, bread cubes, sugar, seasonings and 3 bacon strips,
crumbled. Cover.

Microwave at High 4 to 6 minutes, or until thickened and bubbly,
stirring once or twice. Crumble remaining bacon strip and sprinkle
over casserole.

Variation:
Substitute 1 can (16 oz.) whole tomatoes, chopped, drained and ½
cup liquid reserved, for fresh. Follow directions above, adding
reserved liquid with tomatoes to bread cubes, sugar, seasonings
and bacon.

*Follow photo directions, page 139.

Vegetable Combinations

Two or more vegetables in combination are often more interesting than any one of them alone, because contrast in flavor, color, shape and texture gives them eye and appetite appeal. Unless you combine vegetables with similar cooking times, quick-cooking ingredients should be added toward the end of microwaving. Another technique uses cutting and arranging to equalize energy and cooking times.

Slice long-cooking vegetables thinly and arrange toward the outside of the dish. Cut quicker cooking vegetables in large pieces. Place delicate ones in the center of the dish.

◄ Seasoned Combo Tray

2 medium carrots, sliced
    diagonally
2 cups broccoli flowerets
2 cups cauliflowerets
½ lb. hubbard squash, peeled
    and cut into wedges
1 small zucchini, thinly sliced
2 tablespoons water
1 medium tomato, cut into 6
    wedges
2 tablespoons butter or
    margarine
1 tablespoon grated
    Parmesan cheese
½ teaspoon onion salt

Serves 4

Arrange vegetables as shown in photo beginning with carrot slices, then broccoli and cauliflowerets arranged end on end. Overlap winter squash wedges inside cauliflower-broccoli ring. Arrange zucchini slices in center. Sprinkle tray with 2 tablespoons water. Cover with plastic wrap. Microwave at High 6 to 8 minutes, or until tender-crisp, rotating once.

Arrange tomato wedges on broccoli-cauliflower ring; re-cover. Microwave 1 to 2 minutes, or until vegetables are tender and tomatoes heated. Remove from oven. Let stand covered while preparing sauce.

Place butter in 2-cup measure. Microwave at High 30 to 60 seconds, or until butter melts. Blend in cheese and onion salt. Drain vegetables. Pour sauce over vegetables. Serve as an appetizer or vegetable course.

Italian Vegetable Soup ►

1 medium onion, thinly sliced
    and separated into rings
1 clove garlic, minced or
    pressed
½ cup thinly sliced celery
¼ cup chopped green pepper
1 tablespoon olive or
    vegetable oil
1 can (16 oz.) Northern beans
1 can (16 oz.) stewed
    tomatoes
1 medium zucchini, halved
    lengthwise and thinly
    sliced
½ cup quick-cooking rice
2½ cups water
¼ cup red wine
2 teaspoons parsley flakes
¼ teaspoon salt
¼ teaspoon whole oregano
⅛ teaspoon black pepper
1 bay leaf
2 teaspoons instant beef
    bouillon granules
¼ cup grated Parmesan
    cheese, optional

Serves 8

In 3 to 5-qt. casserole combine onion, garlic, celery, green pepper and oil. Cover; microwave at High 5 to 6 minutes, or until tender, stirring once during cooking.

Add remaining ingredients except cheese. Re-cover. Microwave at High 18 to 20 minutes, or until zucchini is tender and rice is cooked, stirring 2 or 3 times.

Sprinkle individual servings with Parmesan cheese, if desired.

◄ Vegetable Lasagna

8 oz. fresh mushrooms, coarsely chopped
1 green pepper, chopped
1 medium onion, chopped
1 clove garlic, pressed or minced
2 tablespoons olive oil
1 can (16 oz.) whole tomatoes
1 can (16 oz.) tomato paste
⅓ cup red wine or water
1 tablespoon parsley flakes
1½ teaspoons salt, divided
2 teaspoons sugar
1 teaspoon basil leaves
1 teaspoon oregano leaves
2 bay leaves
1 carton (15 oz.) ricotta cheese or 2 cups large-curd cottage cheese
2 eggs
½ cup grated Parmesan cheese, divided
¼ teaspoon black pepper
9 lasagna noodles, cooked
3 cups shredded mozzarella cheese

Serves 8

How to Microwave Vegetable Lasagna

Combine mushrooms, green pepper, onion, garlic and oil in 3-qt. casserole; cover. Microwave at High 6 to 8 minutes, or until tender, stirring once.

Stir in tomatoes, paste, wine, parsley flakes, 1 teaspoon salt, sugar, basil, oregano and bay leaves. Microwave at High, uncovered, 5 minutes; stir.

Reduce power to 50% (Medium). Microwave 30 minutes, or until flavors are blended and mixture is thickened, stirring 2 or 3 times. Remove bay leaves.

Mix together in medium bowl ricotta, eggs, ¼ cup Parmesan, ½ teaspoon salt and black pepper. In 12 × 8-in. baking dish layer one-third each of noodles, ricotta mixture, sauce and mozzarella. Repeat twice; sprinkle with ¼ cup Parmesan.

Microwave at 50% (Medium) 20 minutes, or until hot and bubbly, rotating dish ½ turn once. Let stand 12 minutes to set.

Zucchini & Onions With Tomatoes

3 cups sliced zucchini, ¼-in.
1 small onion, thinly sliced and
     separated into rings
2 tablespoons olive or
     vegetable oil
½ teaspoon salt
½ teaspoon whole oregano
¼ teaspoon marjoram
⅛ teaspoon garlic powder
     Dash pepper
1 tomato, cut into wedges
1 tablespoon grated Parmesan
     cheese, optional

Serves 4 to 6

In 2-qt. casserole combine zucchini, onion, oil and seasonings. Cover. Microwave at High 6 minutes. Stir in tomato wedges; re-cover. Microwave at High 2 to 4 minutes, or until desired tenderness.

Serve with grated Parmesan cheese, if desired.

Spinach, Water Chestnuts & Sprouts

2 tablespoons butter or
     margarine
2 tablespoons soy sauce
⅛ teaspoon ginger
1 lb. fresh spinach
1 cup fresh or canned bean
     sprouts, drained
1 can (8 oz.) sliced water
     chestnuts, drained
⅛ teaspoon pepper
¼ cup chopped green onion

Serves 4

In small dish, microwave butter at High 30 to 60 seconds, or until melted. Stir in soy sauce and ginger. Set aside.

Preheat 10-in. browning dish at High 3 minutes. Add butter mixture, tilting dish to coat bottom. Stir in remaining ingredients. Cover. Microwave at High 2 to 3 minutes, or just until spinach is wilted. Toss to coat spinach well.

Vegetable Chop Suey ▲

2 cups sliced celery
1 cup chopped onion
8 oz. fresh mushrooms, sliced
2 tablespoons butter or
     margarine
½ cup water
3 tablespoons soy sauce
2 tablespoons cornstarch
1 teaspoon instant beef
     bouillon granules
1 teaspoon sugar
1 can (16 oz.) Chinese
     vegetables, drained
⅛ teaspoon pepper

Serves 4 to 6

Mix celery, onion, mushrooms, and butter in 2-qt. casserole; cover. Microwave at High 6 to 8 minutes, or until tender-crisp. Set aside.

In 2-cup measure combine water, soy sauce, cornstarch, bouillon granules and sugar. Microwave at High 2 to 3 minutes, or until thickened, stirring twice during cooking.

Mix sauce and remaining ingredients with celery mixture. Microwave at High 4 to 6 minutes, or until thoroughly heated, stirring after half the time. Serve over rice or chow mein noodles.

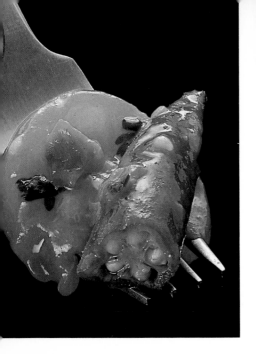

Okra Creole ▲

¾ lb. fresh whole okra
¼ cup water
1 tablespoon cornstarch
1 can (16 oz.) stewed
    tomatoes
2 tablespoons red wine or
    reserved cooking liquid
1 teaspoon parsley flakes
½ teaspoon sugar
¼ teaspoon paprika
⅛ teaspoon garlic powder
    Dash cayenne
    Dash pepper

Serves 4 to 6

In 2-qt. casserole prepare okra
as directed on page 72.
Microwave until tender-crisp;
drain. If desired, reserve liquid
to be used in place of wine.

Mix cornstarch with small
amount of liquid from the
stewed tomatoes until smooth.
Add to okra with remaining ingredients; stir. Cover.
Microwave at High 7 to 8
minutes, or until thickened and
bubbly, stirring once or twice
during cooking.

Variation:
Substitute 1 pkg. (10 oz.) frozen
whole okra for fresh. Prepare as
directed on page 72.

Cashew Peapods ▲

1 pkg. (6 oz.) frozen pea
    pods, defrosted and
    drained
1 can (8 oz.) sliced water
    chestnuts, drained
2 cups fresh sliced
    mushrooms
⅓ cup chopped green onion
2 tablespoons soy sauce
1½ teaspoons cornstarch
1 teaspoon sugar
    Dash garlic powder
    Dash ginger
1 tablespoon butter or
    margarine
¼ cup cashews

Serves 4

In medium bowl combine vegetables, soy sauce, cornstarch,
sugar and seasonings. Let
stand while preheating dish.

Preheat 10-in. browning dish 3
minutes at High. Add butter; tilt
dish to coat bottom. Add vegetable mixture to dish, stirring to
prevent sticking. Cover. Microwave at High 2 to 3 minutes, or
until tender-crisp, stirring after
half the cooking time.

Mix in cashews and serve.

Cream of Vegetable Soup

1 medium potato, peeled and
    cut into ½-in. cubes
1 medium carrot, thinly sliced
1 small onion, chopped
1 cup fresh cut corn
1 cup fresh green peas
1 cup fresh chopped broccoli,
    ½-in. pieces
½ cup water
¼ cup all-purpose flour
¼ teaspoon salt
⅛ teaspoon rosemary, crushed
⅛ teaspoon pepper
2 cups milk
1 can (10¾ oz.) chicken broth
½ cup half and half or
    whipping cream

Makes 1½ quarts

In 3-qt. casserole combine
vegetables and water; cover.
Microwave at High 12 to 14
minutes, or until potato and
carrot are tender, stirring after
half the cooking time.

Mix in flour and seasonings.
Blend in milk and broth.
Microwave at High 12 to 14
minutes, or until thickened,
stirring 3 or 4 times during
cooking. Stir in half and half.

Variation:
Substitute frozen, defrosted
corn, peas and chopped
broccoli for fresh.

Ratatouille ▲

1 medium onion, sliced
1 medium green pepper, cut into strips
1 medium eggplant, peeled and cut into ½-in. cubes
1 clove garlic, minced or pressed
¼ cup olive or vegetable oil
2 medium zucchini, cut into ¼-in. slices
2 teaspoons parsley flakes
1 teaspoon basil leaves
1 teaspoon oregano leaves
1 teaspoon salt
½ teaspoon sugar
⅛ teaspoon black pepper
3 medium tomatoes, peeled and cut into wedges

Serves 6 to 8

In 3-qt. casserole combine onion, green pepper, eggplant, garlic and oil. Cover. Microwave at High 4 to 6 minutes, or until onion is tender and eggplant is translucent.

Stir in remaining ingredients except tomatoes. Cover. Microwave at High 5 to 7 minutes, or until vegetables are almost tender, stirring after half the cooking time.

Gently mix in tomatoes. Cover. Microwave at High 2 minutes, or until tomatoes are heated and vegetables are tender, stirring after half the cooking time.

Vegetable Vinaigrette

2 cups fresh cauliflowerets
1 cup julienne carrots, ¼ × ¼ × 1½ in.
1 cup fresh green beans, cut into 1½-in. pieces
¼ cup water
¾ cup olive or vegetable oil
⅓ cup cider vinegar
2 cloves garlic, halved
1 tablespoon chopped pimiento
2 teaspoons sugar
1 teaspoon chervil
1 teaspoon oregano leaves
1 teaspoon chopped chives
¼ teaspoon salt
⅛ teaspoon pepper
½ cup garbanzo beans, cooked or canned, drained

Serves 6 to 8

In 1½-qt. casserole combine cauliflowerets, carrots, green beans and water. Cover. Microwave at High 5 to 7 minutes, or until tender-crisp, stirring after half the time.

Combine remaining ingredients in small bowl to make vinaigrette. Drain microwaved vegetables; add vinaigrette. Stir to coat. Cover.

Chill in refrigerator 3 to 4 hours.

Vegetable Fried Rice ▲

⅓ cup thinly sliced celery
⅓ cup chopped green pepper
⅓ cup chopped green onion
1 small carrot, chopped
1 can (8½ oz.) bamboo shoots, drained
2 tablespoons oil
1 teaspoon parsley flakes
⅛ teaspoon salt
    Dash pepper
3 tablespoons soy sauce
2 eggs, slightly beaten
2 cups cooked rice

Serves 4

In medium bowl combine vegetables, oil and seasonings. Set aside.

Preheat 10-in. browning dish at High 3 minutes. Add soy sauce all at once. Add vegetable mixture; stir and cover. Microwave at High 2 to 4 minutes, or until tender-crisp. Set aside.

Place eggs in small dish. Microwave at High 1 to 1¼ minutes, or until almost set, stirring after half the time.

Stir rice and eggs into vegetable mixture, breaking up into fine particles. Microwave at High 2 minutes to heat through, stirring after half the time.

Vegetable Dressings & Sauces

A sauce does more than dress up a vegetable for family or company meals. It can give the vegetable a different character, or bring out a subtle, new flavor.

Hot Orange Dressing ▲

¼ cup chopped green onion
⅔ cup vegetable oil
⅓ cup white vinegar
1½ tablespoons sugar
¼ teaspoon celery seed
⅛ teaspoon pepper
1 can (11 oz.) mandarin orange sections, drained
Toasted Almonds, page 36

Makes 1½ cups

In 2-cup measure combine all ingredients except orange sections and almonds. Microwave at High 1 to 2 minutes, or until boiling, stirring twice. Gently stir in oranges. Serve with romaine or leaf lettuce. Sprinkle with toasted almonds.

Bacon Vinegar Dressing

4 slices bacon, quartered
1 small onion, chopped
1 tablespoon cornstarch
⅓ cup brown sugar
  Dash pepper
¼ teaspoon celery seed, optional
⅔ cup water
¼ cup cider vinegar

Makes about 1 cup

Place bacon in 1-qt. casserole. Cover with paper towel. Microwave at High 3½ to 4 minutes, or until crisp, rotating dish ½ turn after half the time. Remove bacon to paper towels to drain. Discard all but 2 tablespoons fat. Add onion to casserole. Microwave, uncovered, at High 1½ to 2 minutes, or until tender.

Add cornstarch, brown sugar and seasonings. Blend in water and vinegar. Microwave at High 3½ to 4 minutes, or until clear and thickened, stirring each minute.

Crumble bacon and add to dressing. Serve immediately over leaf lettuce, spinach or cooked, sliced potatoes.

Sweet & Sour Cream Sauce ▶

2 tablespoons butter or
  margarine
2 tablespoons all-purpose
  flour
1 tablespoon sugar
¼ teaspoon caraway seed,
  optional
⅛ teaspoon salt
  Dash pepper
½ cup whipping cream
¼ cup milk
3 tablespoons vinegar

Makes 1 cup

In 1-qt. measure microwave butter at High 30 to 60 seconds, or until melted. Stir in flour, sugar, caraway, salt and pepper until smooth. Blend in cream and milk.

Microwave at High 2 to 4 minutes, or until thickened, stirring every minute. Mix in vinegar. Serve with cooked cabbage, page 41.

White Sauce

2 tablespoons butter or
  margarine
2 tablespoons all-purpose flour
1 teaspoon chopped chives
¼ teaspoon salt
⅛ teaspoon pepper
1 cup milk

Makes 1 cup

Melt butter in 1-qt. measure at High 30 to 60 seconds. Stir in flour and seasonings until smooth. Blend in milk. Microwave at High 2½ to 6 minutes, or until mixture thickens; stir after 2 minutes, then every minute. Serve with sliced potatoes.

Variation:
Cheese Sauce: Add 1 cup shredded Cheddar or American cheese, 1 tablespoon sherry, and ¼ teaspoon dry mustard to hot white sauce. Stir until cheese melts. Microwave at High 30 seconds. Stir before serving. Serve with broccoli, cauliflower or Brussels sprouts.

Tomato Sauce

2 tablespoons chopped onion
2 tablespoons chopped green
  pepper
2 tablespoons butter or
  margarine
1 can (6 oz.) tomato paste
1 teaspoon sugar
¼ teaspoon whole oregano
⅛ teaspoon basil
⅛ teaspoon garlic powder
⅛ teaspoon salt
  Dash pepper
1 cup tomato juice

Makes 1¼ cups

In 1-qt. measure or casserole combine onion, green pepper and butter. Microwave at High 1 to 2 minutes, or until tender.

Stir in tomato paste, sugar and seasonings until smooth. Blend in tomato juice. Microwave at High 3 to 4 minutes, or until hot and bubbly, stirring after half the cooking time. Serve over noodles, poultry or cabbage.

Hollandaise Sauce

2 egg yolks
2 tablespoons lemon juice
  Dash cayenne pepper
½ cup butter or margarine

Makes ⅔ cup

In small bowl combine egg yolks, lemon juice and cayenne.

In small bowl, microwave butter at High 45 to 60 seconds, or until melted. With whisk or fork, stir egg yolk mixture into butter.

Reduce power to 50% (Medium). Microwave 1 to 1½ minutes, or until thickened, stirring every 30 seconds. Stir before serving. Serve with asparagus.

Variation:
Mousseline Sauce: Cool sauce to room temperature. Fold in ¼ cup whipped cream. Serve with broccoli, cauliflower or spinach.

Fruits

Frozen Fruit

Frozen fruits are available in a variety of forms. Individually quick frozen fruits are unsweetened and packaged in large plastic bags. You can remove as much fruit as you wish and return the rest to the freezer. Sweetened fruits are packaged in pouches for quick defrosting, in boxes, which may have metal ends, and in plastic containers.

Fruits are usually defrosted only until a few pieces feel warm. After standing, the fruit should be cold, firm and slightly icy. It is then ready to serve or use in one of these recipes.

How to Defrost Frozen Fruits

Bags. Measure amount needed into bowl or measure. Microwave at 50% (Medium) until a few pieces feel warm, stirring after half the defrosting time. Stir again and let stand 5 minutes.

Pouches. Flex pouch to break up fruit. With knife, cut large 'X' in pouch. Place cut side down in 1-qt. casserole or serving dish. Microwave at High until outer fruit feels slightly warm. Lift far corners of pouch to release fruit into dish. Stir; let stand 5 minutes.

Defrosting Fruit Chart

Type	Amount	Microwave Time at High	Procedure
Bags Blackberries, Blueberries, Cherries, Cranberries, Peaches, Raspberries, Rhubarb	1 cup	1-3 min.	Follow photo directions. 2-cup measure. Stir once.
	2 cups	2½-5 min.	1-qt. casserole. Stir twice.
	4 cups	5-8 min	2-qt. casserole. Stir twice
Quick Thaw Pouch Peaches, Raspberries, Strawberries	10 oz. pkg.	2-3 min.	Follow photo directions.
Box with metal ends Strawberries, Raspberries	10 oz. pkg. 16 oz. pkg.	2 min. 2-3 min.	Follow photo directions.
Plastic Container Strawberries	16 oz.	3 min. then ½-1 min. longer	Follow photo directions.

Boxes. If box has metal ends, remove one end and set package upright in oven. Place all-paper box unopened in bowl. Microwave at High until outer berries or paper carton feel slightly warm. Let stand 10 to 12 minutes. Pour fruit into bowl. Stir carefully to break up any icy portions.

Plastic container. Run hot water over container to loosen fruit. Place fruit in bowl. Microwave at High 3 minutes. Let stand 5 minutes; break up icy portions. Microwave 30 to 60 seconds, or until able to separate. Let stand 5 minutes.

Apples

There are at least a dozen varieties of apple which are popular nation-wide, plus many more local varieties. At least one of them will be in its peak season any month of the year.

Microwaving retains the fresh flavor and texture of apples. Choosing the right variety for pies, baking or sauces is important. Use your favorite cooking apple, or follow your grocer's suggestions. Large apples are attractive for fruit bowls or baking, but smaller ones may provide better flavor and texture and be more economical in pies and sauces.

How to Select Apples

Choose apples which are firm, smooth-skinned and free of bruises or punctures. Color should be bright, but will differ with the variety. Pictured left to right, front row: Golden Delicious, Greening, McIntosh, varieties good for cooking. Back row: Rome, Winesap, Delicious, popular varieties for eating raw.

How to Store Apples

Store apples in a plastic container in the refrigerator to retain flavor and crispness. Use as desired.

Rosy Apple Sauce

8 medium cooking apples, peeled, cored and chopped
2 tablespoons water
¼ cup red hots
¼ cup brown sugar
Dash nutmeg

Makes 2½ cups

Combine apples and water in 2-qt. casserole. Cover. Microwave at High 10 to 12 minutes, or until apples are tender, stirring once every 3 minutes.

Stir in red hots, brown sugar and nutmeg. Cover. Microwave at High 2 to 4 minutes, or until red hots are completely dissolved, stirring every minute.

Apple Stuffing

2 medium cooking apples, cored and chopped
1 medium onion, chopped
1 medium stalk celery, chopped
3 tablespoons butter or margarine
¼ cup water
1 teaspoon instant chicken bouillon granules
3 cups dry unseasoned bread cubes
1 teaspoon parsley flakes
½ teaspoon poultry seasoning
¼ teaspoon salt
⅛ teaspoon pepper
⅓ cup chopped nuts
¼ cup raisins

Makes about 4 cups

In 1½ to 2-qt. casserole combine apples, onion, celery and butter. Cover; microwave at High 4 to 5 minutes, or until mixture is tender.

In 1-cup measure microwave water at High 45 to 60 seconds or until boiling. Dissolve bouillon in water. Add to apple mixture.

Stir in bread and seasonings. Add nuts and raisins. Cover; microwave at High 1 minute to soften bread crumbs.

Apple Pie ▲

1 microwaved 9-in. pie shell
   with cut outs, opposite
5 cups peeled, cored and
   sliced cooking apples
1 tablespoon lemon juice
⅓ cup white sugar
⅓ cup brown sugar
3 tablespoons all-purpose
   flour
½ teaspoon cinnamon

Makes 9-in. pie

Place apples in a large bowl. Toss with lemon juice. Combine sugars, flour and cinnamon. Sprinkle over apples; toss to coat.

Spoon apple mixture into prepared crust. Place in oven on wax paper. Microwave at High 8 to 11 minutes, or until apples are tender. Prepare cut outs with reserved pastry, following directions, opposite. Top pie with cut outs.

One Crust Pie Shell

⅓ cup shortening
2 tablespoons butter or
   margarine, softened
1 cup all-purpose or
   whole wheat flour
½ teaspoon salt
3 tablespoons cold water
3 or 4 drops yellow food
   coloring, optional

Makes 9-in. pie shell

One Crust Pie Shell With Cut Outs

⅓ cup plus 2½ tablespoons
   shortening
3 tablespoons butter or
   margarine, softened
1½ cups all-purpose or whole
   wheat flour
¾ teaspoon salt
4½ tablespoons cold water
4 to 5 drops yellow food
   coloring, optional

Makes 9-in. pie
shell and cut outs

Cut shortening and butter into flour and salt until particles resemble small peas. Combine water and food coloring. Sprinkle over flour mixture; stir until particles are just moist enough to cling together and form a ball. Set aside one-third dough if making cut outs.

Roll dough out on floured cloth to ⅛-in. thick circle 2 inches larger than inverted pie plate. Fit into pie plate. Microwave at High 5 to 7 minutes, rotating dish ½ turn every 3 minutes. Check for doneness through bottom of pie plate. Crust will not brown, but will appear dry and opaque.

For cut outs, roll out dough and cut reserved dough into 6 pieces with cookie cutter, or make one 6 or 7-in. circle. Prick with fork to mark 6 wedges. Sprinkle with 1 teaspoon sugar and ⅛ teaspoon cinnamon; transfer to wax paper. Arrange cookie shapes in ring. Microwave at High 2 to 4 minutes, or until dry and puffy, rotating every minute. Watch closely. Roll pastry for lattice to 8-in. circle on wax paper, cut into ten or twelve ½-in. wide strips. Microwave as directed for cut outs. Loosen from wax paper while warm.

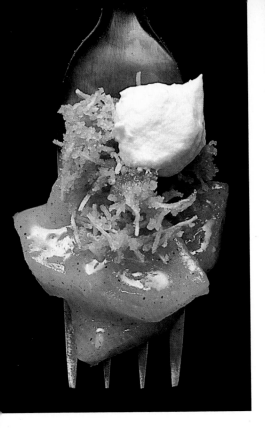

Apple Crisp ▲

6 cups peeled, cored and
   sliced cooking apples
1 tablespoon lemon juice
½ cup sugar
½ teaspoon cinnamon
2 tablespoons all-purpose flour

Topping:
¾ cup all-purpose flour
¾ cup brown sugar
¼ teaspoon nutmeg
1 teaspoon cinnamon
⅓ cup butter or margarine
2 large shredded wheat
   biscuits, crumbled

Makes 8 × 8-in. dish

In mixing bowl combine apples,
lemon juice, sugar, cinnamon
and flour. Spread mixture evenly
in 8 × 8-in. baking dish.

Combine all topping ingredients
except butter and wheat biscuits. Cut in butter with fork or
pastry blender until crumbly. Stir
in crumbled wheat biscuits.
Sprinkle over apples. Microwave
at High 8 to 13 minutes, or until
apples are tender and bubbly,
rotating dish ½ turn after half
the time. Serve with whipped
cream, if desired.

Caramel Apples ▲

6 medium Red Delicious
   or McIntosh apples
1 cup chopped dry roasted
   peanuts
1 bag (14 oz.) caramels
2 tablespoons water

Makes 6 apples

Wash and dry apples. Insert
stick in stem end. Place
chopped peanuts in a small
bowl. Set aside. Place
unwrapped caramels and water
in a 1-qt. casserole. Microwave
at High 3 to 4 minutes, or until
melted, hot and bubbly, stirring
every minute.

Dip apples in hot caramel
mixture and then roll in
chopped peanuts. Let cool on
wax paper.

Variation:
Substitute 1 cup finely chopped
cashews, pecans or walnuts for
the chopped peanuts.

Baked Apples

4 cooking apples
2 tablespoons brown sugar
2 tablespoons orange juice
   concentrate
¼ cup apple juice
3 tablespoons raisins
½ to 1 teaspoon cinnamon

Serves 4

Core apples; peel a strip of
apple skin one-third down
around apple to allow steam to
escape. Blend brown sugar,
orange juice concentrate, apple
juice, raisins, and cinnamon.

Place apples in 9-in. round or
8 × 8-in. baking dish, leaving
center empty. Pour apple juice
and brown sugar mixture
around apples. Cover with
plastic wrap. Microwave at High
6 to 7 minutes, or until almost
tender, spooning sauce over
apples and rotating dish ½ turn
after half the cooking time. Let
stand 2 to 3 minutes.

Serve in individual dishes with
the sauce.

Bananas & Plantains

Bananas and plantains ripen best after picking, so you can buy them slightly green. Use firm, green tipped bananas for cooking, yellow ones for eating raw, and brown flecked fruit to mash for banana bread or milkshakes. Starchier than bananas, plantains are cooked as a vegetable and should be well ripened before using.

How to Select & Store Bananas & Plantains

Look for plump bananas that are not bruised or split. Plantains are larger and stubbier than bananas. When ripe, they have brown skin, dark spots and rough areas.

Leave bananas and plantains uncovered at room temperature. Refrigerate bananas after they reach desired ripeness; then use within a day or two. Do not refrigerate plantains.

Bananas Foster

¼ cup butter or margarine
¼ cup brown sugar
½ teaspoon cinnamon
¼ teaspoon nutmeg
3 or 4 medium bananas
1 to 2 tablespoons banana
    liqueur
1 to 2 tablespoons light rum

              Serves 6

Peel bananas. Slice lengthwise and then crosswise once to quarter. Set aside.

In 2-qt. casserole melt butter at High 1 to 1½ minutes. Stir in sugar and spices. Microwave at High 30 to 60 seconds, or until hot. Gently mix in bananas. Microwave at High 1 minute.

Microwave banana liqueur and rum in small dish at High 20 seconds to warm. Pour into ladle; ignite and pour over bananas. Serve over ice cream.

Brown Sugar Baked Plantains

2 very ripe large plantains
2 tablespoons lemon juice
¼ cup brown sugar

              Serves 4

Peel plantains. Slice lengthwise and then crosswise to quarter.

Place lemon juice in medium bowl. Dip each plantain quarter in juice. Set aside. Spread brown sugar on wax paper. Roll pieces in brown sugar to coat.

Arrange plantains on microwave roasting rack. Microwave at High 2 to 3 minutes, or until softened and heated through.

Banana Pie

Crust:
¼ cup plus 1 tablespoon
    butter or margarine
1⅓ cup fine graham cracker or
    vanilla cookie crumbs
2 tablespoons brown or
    granulated sugar

Filling:
½ cup sugar
3 tablespoons cornstarch
⅛ teaspoon salt
2 cups milk
3 egg yolks, slightly beaten
1 tablespoon butter or
    margarine
1 teaspoon vanilla
2 ripe medium bananas

         Makes 9-in. pie

To prepare crust, melt butter in 9-in. pie plate at High 1 to 1½ minutes. Stir in crumbs and sugar. Reserve 2 tablespoons crumb mixture for garnish, if desired. Press crumbs firmly and evenly against bottom and sides of plate. Microwave at High 1½ minutes, rotating ½ turn after 1 minute. Set aside.

Combine sugar, cornstarch and salt in 2-qt. casserole. Stir in milk. Microwave at High 6 to 7 minutes, or until thickened, stirring every 2 to 3 minutes. Stir about ½ cup mixture into yolks. Return to mixture in casserole, stirring constantly. Microwave at High 1½ minutes, or until thickened. Mix in butter. Cool slightly; stir in vanilla. Cover with wax paper or plastic wrap to prevent skin from forming. Cool to room temperature.

Peel and slice bananas; arrange in bottom of microwaved pie shell. Pour in filling. Chill pie thoroughly. Serve with sweetened whipped cream, if desired.

Berries

Some strawberries are available year-round, but the peak season is April through June. Blueberries are in best supply June through August, while the raspberry and blackberry season is June and July. Cranberries appear September through December.

When fresh berries are not in season, substitute berries frozen without syrup for use in recipes. Measure the berries frozen, then defrost and drain, except cranberries which should be rinsed, then cooked from the frozen state.

Strawberry Pie ▲

1 microwaved 9-in. pie shell, page 118
1½ qts. fresh strawberries, divided
3 tablespoons cornstarch
¾ to 1 cup sugar (depends on sweetness of strawberries)
1 cup water
4 to 5 drops red food coloring, optional

Makes 9-in pie

Clean and hull berries. Mash enough berries to measure ⅔ cup. Combine cornstarch and sugar in 1 to 1½-qt. casserole. Stir in water and mashed berries. Microwave at High 5 to 6 minutes, or until thick and bubbly, stirring every other minute. Cool. Stir in food coloring, if desired.

Place remaining berries in prepared pie shell. Pour cooled glaze evenly over top. Chill about 3 hours, or until set. If desired, serve with whipped cream.

How to Store Berries

Refrigerate cranberries in the original plastic bag and use within a week or two, or freeze them in the bag and use when desired. All other berries, including strawberries, raspberries, blackberries and blueberries, are highly perishable; they should be used within 2 or 3 days.

To store, place unwashed berries in a single layer in a shallow container, discarding bruised or decayed ones. Lay a paper towel on top of the berries, then cover and refrigerate. Do not wash berries until ready to use. Hull strawberries after washing.

How to Select Berries

Raspberries and Blackberries range in color from golden to red, purple and black. They should be cold and dry. Avoid berries which show signs of mold, bruising or leaking.

Blueberries should be dark blue with a silvery bloom, plump, firm, dry and free from stems and leaves. Large berries are preferred.

Strawberries should be clean, with solid bright red color, few green or white spots, and a well attached cap. Very small or large berries lack the flavor of medium-sized ones; large berries may be hollow. Check containers for signs of leakage, moisture and mold.

Cranberries are selected for quality before they are packed, so the berries should be firm, plump, shiny red to reddish black. Poor quality berries are sticky, dull, soft or shriveled.

Blueberry Pie ▲

1 microwaved 9-in. pie shell,
    page 118

Filling:
3 cups blueberries, fresh
    or frozen, defrosted,
    page 115, drained
½ cup sugar
¼ cup all-purpose flour

½ teaspoon grated lemon peel
¼ teaspoon cinnamon
¼ teaspoon nutmeg

Topping:
½ cup quick-cooking rolled oats
2 tablespoons butter
2 tablespoons brown sugar
½ teaspoon cinnamon

Makes 9-in. pie

In medium bowl combine filling ingredients. Turn into shell. Cut
topping ingredients together with fork or pastry blender. Sprinkle
on top of filling. Place pie on wax paper in oven.

Microwave at High 5 minutes. Rotate ¼ turn. Reduce power to
50% (Medium). Microwave 3 to 11 minutes, or until filling is bubbly
and thickened, rotating ¼ turn every 3 minutes.

Variation:
Substitute 4 cups frozen, defrosted and drained raspberries or
blackberries for blueberries; increase sugar to ⅔ cup.

Blueberry Melba Sauce

1½ tablespoons cornstarch
  1 tablespoon sugar
  1 pkg. (10 oz.) frozen
    sweetened raspberries,
    defrosted, page 115

½ cup red currant jelly
1 cup blueberries, fresh or
  frozen, defrosted,
  page 115

Makes 2 cups

In 1 to 1½-qt. casserole combine cornstarch and sugar. Stir in
raspberries and jelly. Microwave at High 3 to 4 minutes, or until
mixture is clear and thickened, stirring every other minute. Strain
and cool. Mix in blueberries. If desired, place a peach half with ice
cream in sherbet dishes. Top with blueberry sauce.

Blueberry Muffins

1¾ cups all-purpose flour
 ⅓ cup sugar
 ¾ teaspoon salt
 2 teaspoons baking powder
 2 eggs
 ¾ cup buttermilk
 ¼ cup vegetable oil
 ½ teaspoon vanilla
 1 teaspoon grated lemon
    peel
 1 cup blueberries, fresh or
    frozen, defrosted,
    page 115, drained

Topping:
2 tablespoons sugar
½ teaspoon cinnamon

Makes 14 to 16 muffins

In large bowl combine dry
ingredients. In smaller bowl
beat together eggs, buttermilk
and oil with whisk or fork. Pour
liquid mixture into dry mixture,
mixing only until particles are
moistened. Fold in vanilla,
lemon peel and blueberries.

Line custard cups or microwave
cupcake dish with 2 paper
liners. Fill cups half full; don't
overfill. Sprinkle with cinnamon
and sugar mixture.

If using custard cups, arrange
in a ring when microwaving 3 or
more muffins at a time.
Microwave at High as directed
in chart. Rotate muffins after half
the time. Remove muffins from
cups to wire rack after baking.

1 muffin	½ to ¾ min.
2 muffins	¾ to 1½ min.
4 muffins	1 to 2 min.
6 muffins	1½ to 2½ min.

Blueberry Jam ▲

1½ pints fresh blueberries,
    washed and drained
1 tablespoon lemon juice
½ teaspoon lemon peel
½ box (1¾ oz.) powdered fruit
    pectin*
2½ cups sugar

Makes 3 cups

In 2-qt. measure or 3-qt.
casserole mash berries. Stir in
lemon juice, peel, and pectin.
Microwave at High 10 to 12
minutes, or until mixture comes
to a full rolling boil around
edges and in center. Stir twice
during cooking. Stir in sugar.
Microwave at High 5 to 7
minutes, or until mixture comes
to a full rolling boil, stirring after
half the time. Boil 1 minute.

Store mixture in refrigerator or
pour into hot sterilized jars, seal
and process.

*Measure and divide pectin in
half accurately. Reserve half for
later use.

Quick Raspberry Jam ▲

2 pkgs. (10 oz. each) frozen
    sweetened raspberries,
    defrosted but still
    slightly frozen, page 115
1 tablespoon lime juice
½ teaspoon lime peel
½ box (1¾ oz.) powdered fruit
    pectin*
2 cups sugar

Makes 2½ cups

In 2-qt. measure or 3-qt.
casserole combine berries,
juice, peel and pectin. Microwave at High 9½ to 12 minutes,
or until mixture comes to a full
rolling boil around edges and in
center. Stir twice during
cooking. Stir in sugar.
Microwave at High 3½ to 6
minutes, or until mixture comes
to a full rolling boil, stirring after
half the time. Boil 1 minute.

Store mixture in refrigerator or
pour into hot sterilized jars, seal
and process.

*Measure and divide pectin in
half accurately. Reserve half for
later use.

Freezer Strawberry Jam ▲

1 qt. fresh ripe strawberries,
    cleaned and hulled (about
    2½ cups mashed berries)
½ box (1¾ oz.) powdered fruit
    pectin*
3 cups sugar

Makes 3½ cups

Slice strawberries into 2-qt.
measure or 3-qt. casserole.
Mash well. Stir in pectin
thoroughly. Microwave at High 6
to 10 minutes, or until mixture
comes to a full rolling boil,
around edges and in center,
stirring after half the time.

Mix in sugar well. Microwave at
High 4 to 6½ minutes, or until
mixture comes to a full rolling
boil, stirring after 3 minutes,
then every minute to prevent
boil over. Boil mixture 1 minute.
Store mixture in refrigerator or
pour into hot sterilized jars, seal
and process.

*Measure and divide pectin in
half accurately. Reserve half for
later use.

Variation:
Substitute 1¼ pkgs. (16 oz.
each) frozen unsweetened
whole strawberries, defrosted,
page 115 (but still slightly
frozen) for fresh.

Cranberry-Apple Relish

1 cup sugar
¼ teaspoon ground cloves
¼ teaspoon cinnamon
¼ teaspoon allspice
½ cup apple juice
1 lb. whole cranberries fresh or
   frozen, defrosted, page 115
1 medium apple, cored and
   chopped
½ cup chopped walnuts

Makes 1½ qts.

Combine sugar, spices and
apple juice in 1½ to 2-qt.
casserole. Stir to blend. Add
cranberries and apple. Cover.

Microwave at High 9 to 11
minutes, or until skins of berries
just begin to split and liquid is
slightly thickened.

Stir in walnuts. Let relish cool
before serving.

◄Cranberry-Pineapple Bread

1¼ cups all-purpose flour
1 cup brown sugar
⅓ cup shortening
1 tablespoon vegetable oil
2 large eggs
½ cup walnuts, chopped
½ cup shredded coconut
1 teaspoon vanilla extract
1 teaspoon baking powder
1 teaspoon baking soda
½ teaspoon salt
1 cup quartered
   cranberries, fresh or
   frozen, defrosted, page 115
1 can (8 oz.) crushed
   pineapple*

Topping:

2 tablespoons confectioners'
   sugar, optional
¼ cup shredded coconut,
   optional

Makes 9 × 5-in. loaf

Place all ingredients in large
mixing bowl. Blend at low
speed until all ingredients are
moistened. Beat at medium
speed 2 minutes.

Spread batter in 9 × 5-in. loaf
dish lined on bottom with wax
paper. Shield ends of loaf dish
with 2-in. wide strips of foil,
covering 1 inch of batter and
molding remainder around
handles of loaf dish.

Center loaf dish on inverted
saucer in oven. Microwave at
50% (Medium) 9 minutes,
rotating ¼ turn every 1 to 2
minutes. Increase power to
High; microwave 2 to 4 minutes.
Remove foil after 2 minutes, and
rotate every 1 to 2 minutes.

Dust cooled loaf with
confectioners' sugar or sprinkle
with coconut during last cooking
stage, if desired.

*When using fresh cranberries,
drain pineapple and use only ¼
cup of the liquid.

Raspberry Cobbler

2 cups fresh raspberries
¾ cup sugar, divided
1½ tablespoons cornstarch
1 cup all-purpose flour
1½ teaspoons baking powder
¼ teaspoon salt
2 tablespoons butter or
   margarine
⅓ cup plus 1 tablespoon milk
1 tablespoon butter or
   margarine, melted
¾ teaspoon cinnamon

Serves 4

In 1-qt. casserole combine
raspberries, ½ cup sugar and
cornstarch. Microwave at High
3 to 6 minutes, or until mixture
is clear and thickened, stirring
2 or 3 times. Set aside.

In medium bowl combine flour,
baking powder, salt and 2
tablespoons sugar. Cut 2 tablespoons butter into flour mixture
with a pastry blender until fine
particles form. Add milk; stir
only until dough clings together.
Knead 4 or 5 times on floured
surface until dough is smooth
and elastic. Roll dough into
8 × 9-in. rectangle. Brush with
1 tablespoon melted butter
and sprinkle with mixture of
2 tablespoons sugar and
the cinnamon.

Cut dough into six 1½-in.
wide strips. Roll up each strip
sweet roll style and arrange on
top of raspberry mixture around
the outer edge, leaving center
area empty.

Microwave at High 3½ to 4
minutes, or until biscuits spring
back when touched, rotating ¼
turn every minute.

Variation:

Substitute 1 bag (12 oz.) frozen
raspberries, defrosted, page 115,
drained, for fresh raspberries.

Raspberry Cream Torte ▶

Vanilla Filling:
¼ cup sugar
2½ tablespoons cornstarch
Pinch salt
1¼ cups milk
3 egg yolks, slightly beaten
1 tablespoon butter or margarine
1 teaspoon vanilla

Pastry:
2 cups all-purpose flour
½ teaspoon salt
⅓ cup butter or margarine
⅓ cup shortening
¼ to ½ cup whipping cream
4 to 5 drops yellow food coloring

Raspberry Filling:
1 pkg. (10 oz.) frozen raspberries, defrosted, page 115, drained and juice reserved
1½ tablespoons cornstarch

Serves 6 to 8

Prepare fillings and pastry as directed. To assemble torte place one pastry ring on serving plate. Spread with one-third vanilla cream mixture, then one-fourth raspberry filling. Repeat twice, ending with pastry. Top with remaining raspberry filling.

Vanilla Cream Filling:
In medium bowl combine sugar, cornstarch and salt. Gradually stir in milk. Microwave at High 4 to 7 minutes, or until very thick, stirring after 2 minutes, then every minute. Mix a little hot mixture into egg yolks. Blend into remaining milk mixture. Reduce power to 50% (Medium). Microwave 1 minute. Stir in butter until smooth. Cover; cool slightly. Stir in vanilla. Set aside.

Pastry:
In medium bowl, combine flour and salt. Cut in butter and shortening until particles resemble coarse crumbs or small peas. Combine whipping cream and food coloring. Sprinkle over mixture while tossing with a fork, until particles are just moist enough to cling together and form a ball. Divide into 4 equal balls.

Roll each ball on a lightly floured surface into a circle larger than an inverted 7-in. salad plate. Trim around edge of salad plate to form circle. Transfer to wax paper and microwave at High 1½ to 2½ minutes, or until pastry appears dry and opaque. Remove to cooling rack and cool completely. Carefully peel wax paper from pastry. Set aside.

Raspberry Filling:
In small bowl combine reserved juice and cornstarch. Microwave at High 1½ to 2 minutes, or until clear and thickened. Gently stir in berries. Refrigerate until completely cool.

Variation:
Substitute 1 cup fresh raspberries, divided for frozen raspberries. In small bowl mash ½ cup raspberries. Stir in cornstarch, ½ cup water and 2 tablespoons sugar. Microwave as directed above.

Cherries

Most cherries, in the market late May through August, are the sweet, eating varieties. Tart red cherries, used only for cooking, are rarely found in the fresh form. For many recipes, frozen or canned cherries are convenient, because they are already pitted.

How to Select Cherries

Look for firm, ripe, brightly colored cherries. Sweet varieties may be bright red to black, white or golden. Avoid fruit which is sticky, soft, or shows brown spots and skin splits. Overly ripe cherries appear dull, shriveled or leaking, and stems fall out easily. Immature cherries are small, hard, light in color and will not ripen.

How to Store Cherries

Remove cherries from carton and discard any bruised fruit. Pat dry with paper towel to remove condensation, as moisture causes mold. Place in shallow container in a single layer. Lay paper towel on top; cover and refrigerate. Cherries keep 3 to 5 days. Wash just before using.

Cherry Pie ▶

1 microwaved 9-in. pie shell
    with cut outs, page 118
4 cups fresh cherries, pitted
    or 2 cans (16 oz. each)
    pitted red tart cherries,
    water pack, drained
1 cup sugar
¼ cup cornstarch

Makes 9-in. pie

In large bowl combine cherries,
sugar and cornstarch.
Microwave at High 8½ to 10½
minutes, or until mixture is clear
and thickened, stirring every 2
minutes during cooking time.
Let cool slightly. Fill prepared
shell with filling.

Prepare lattice top as directed,
page 118.

Cherry Preserves

4 cups chopped sweet pitted
    cherries, fresh or frozen,
    defrosted, page 115,
    juice reserved
2½ cups sugar
½ box (1¾ oz.) powdered fruit
    pectin*
1 teaspoon lemon juice

Makes 1½ cups

Combine cherries, reserved
juice if using frozen cherries,
sugar and pectin in 3-qt.
casserole. Microwave at High 9
to 13 minutes, or until mixture
boils rapidly. Stir.

Reduce power to 50% (Medium).
Microwave 15 to 20 minutes, or
until mixture thickens slightly
and coats spoon, stirring every
5 minutes. (It will continue to
thicken as it cools.) Stir in lemon
juice. Skim off foam.

Store mixture in refrigerator or
pour into hot sterilized jars, seal
and process.

*Measure and divide pectin in
half accurately. Reserve half for
later use.

Cherry Almond Sauce ▶

¼ cup sugar
1½ tablespoons cornstarch
1 can (16 oz.) pitted dark
    sweet cherries in heavy
    syrup, drained and juice
    reserved
¼ teaspoon almond extract
Toasted Almonds, page 36

Serves 6 to 8

Combine sugar and cornstarch
in 1 to 1½-qt. casserole. Stir in
cherry juice. Microwave at High
2½ to 3½ minutes, or until
bubbly and thickened, stirring
twice during cooking.

Mix in cherries. Microwave at
High 30 seconds to heat. Stir in
almond extract.

Serve over ice cream or
shortcake with whipped cream.
Top with almonds.

129

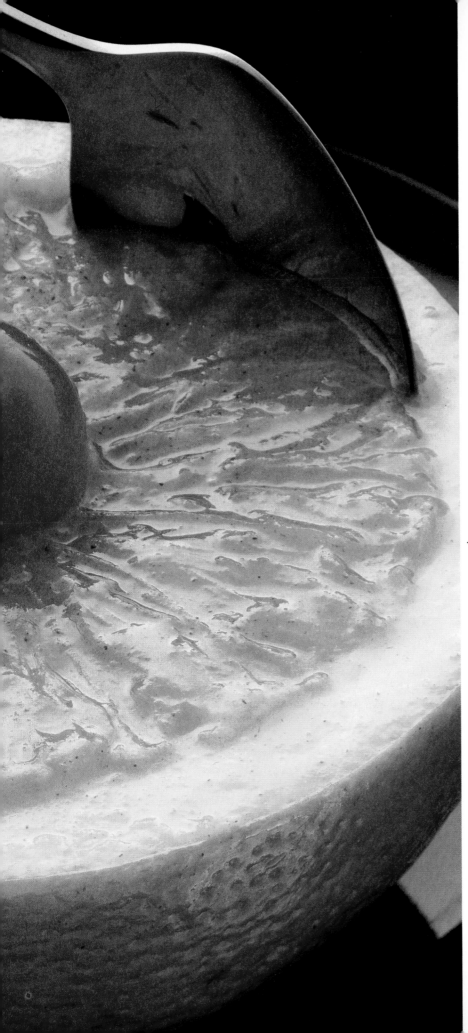

Citrus Fruits

Grapefruit, lemons and limes are available all year. Navel oranges are plentiful November to May, while the Valencia season is February to November.

To get more juice from lemons, limes and oranges, microwave at High 20 to 35 seconds before cutting and squeezing.

How to Store Citrus Fruits

Citrus fruits keep well at room temperature for 7 to 10 days, or refrigerated for 2 to 3 weeks.

◄ Broiled Grapefruit

2 large grapefruit, cut into halves
3 tablespoons butter or margarine
¼ cup brown sugar
¼ teaspoon cinnamon

Serves 4

Remove seeds from grapefruit. Cut around edges and sections to loosen. Place on roasting rack or in serving bowls.

Melt butter in small bowl at High 30 to 45 seconds. Stir in brown sugar and cinnamon. Spoon mixture evenly over grapefruit.

Microwave at High 6 to 7 minutes, or until thoroughly heated, rearranging and rotating grapefruit after half the time.

Variation:
Mix in ½ cup slightly crushed whole wheat flakes with brown sugar and cinnamon.

How to Select Citrus Fruits

Look for fruit which is moderately firm and heavy for its size. Finely textured, thin-skinned fruit is juiciest. Surface scars, caused by fruit brushing against branches, do not affect flavor.

Avoid discolored areas at stem end, soft spots, mold and skin punctures. Spongy texture and dull, dry skin that is wrinkled or hardening indicate age.

Grapefruit may be white or pink fleshed. Skin color ranges from pale yellow to russet. If pointed at stem end, grapefruit is likely to be thick-skinned.

Oranges with green skin color are ripe and sweet inside. Late in the ripening season Valencia oranges tend to develop a greenish skin color. Valencia, or juice oranges and navel, seedless oranges are the main varieties available.

Lemons with pale or greenish yellow skin are slightly more acid than deep yellow lemons. Room temperature is better for lemons than refrigeration.

Limes may be the sweeter Mexican and Florida type with leathery-smooth, light yellow skin or the large bright green, acidic Tahiti. Purple or brown skin spots do not affect flavor.

Orange Squares ▲

¾ cup all-purpose flour
½ cup brown sugar
¼ cup butter or margarine,
    room temperature
¼ cup orange juice
¼ cup dairy sour cream
1 egg
2 teaspoons grated
    orange peel
½ teaspoon baking soda
¼ teaspoon salt

Orange Frosting:
2 tablespoons orange juice
2 tablespoons butter
    or margarine
1 teaspoon grated
    orange peel
1½ to 1¾ cups confectioners'
    sugar
¼ cup chopped cashews

Makes 8 × 8-in. dish

Combine all ingredients except frosting in mixing bowl. Beat at low speed of electric mixer 1 minute, or until well blended. Spread in 8 × 8-in. baking dish.

Place dish on inverted saucer. Microwave at High 4 to 5½ minutes, rotating ¼ turn after 2, 4 and 5 minutes. Check through bottom of dish for doneness. No unbaked batter should appear in center. Cool directly on countertop. Frost with Orange Frosting.

To prepare frosting, combine juice, butter and peel in mixing bowl. Add sugar; beat until smooth and of spreading consistency. Frost cake; sprinkle with chopped cashews.

Orange Sauce ▲

¼ cup sugar
1 tablespoon cornstarch
⅔ cup orange juice
⅓ cup water
2 tablespoons butter
    or margarine
1 tablespoon orange peel
2 teaspoons lemon juice

Makes 1 cup

In 1-qt. casserole combine sugar and cornstarch. Stir in orange juice. Microwave at High 2 to 2¾ minutes, or until thickened, stirring 2 or 3 times during cooking.

Mix in remaining ingredients. Serve warm over gingerbread or cake.

Lime Pie

1 microwaved 9-in. pie shell,
   page 118
1 cup sugar
¼ cup cornstarch
⅛ teaspoon salt
1 cup water, divided
3 egg yolks, slightly beaten
2 tablespoons butter
   or margarine
¼ cup lime juice
2 to 3 drops green food
   coloring, optional

Meringue:
3 egg whites
½ teaspoon cream of tartar
5 tablespoons sugar

Makes 9-in. pie

In mixing bowl or 1½ to 2-qt. casserole combine sugar, cornstarch, salt and ¼ cup water. Stir in remaining water. Microwave at High 5½ to 6 minutes, or until thickened and clear, stirring every 2 minutes.

Mix a small amount of hot mixture into egg yolks. Blend into remaining hot mixture. Microwave at High 1 minute. Stir in butter, juice and coloring. Cool slightly; pour into shell.

Beat egg whites and cream of tartar in small mixing bowl until soft mounds form. Add sugar, a tablespoon at a time, continuing to beat until stiff peaks form.

Spread over filling, sealing to crust edge. Sprinkle lightly with graham cracker crumbs, if desired. Reduce power to 50% (Medium). Microwave 3 to 6 minutes, or until meringue is set, rotating ½ turn after half the time. Refrigerate.

NOTE: For a browned meringue, reduce microwave time to 3 to 4 minutes. Then place under conventional broiler 2 to 4 minutes, watching closely.

Lemon Cheese Pie ▲

5 tablespoons butter
   or margarine
1⅓ cups graham cracker
   crumbs
2 tablespoons white or
   brown sugar

1 pkg. (8 oz.) cream cheese
2 eggs
½ cup sugar
3 tablespoons lemon juice
1 tablespoon lemon peel
¾ cup dairy sour cream

Makes 9-in. pie

Melt butter in 9-in. pie plate at High 45 to 60 seconds. Stir in crumbs and sugar. Remove 1 tablespoon of crumb mixture and set aside. Press crumbs firmly and evenly against bottom and side of plate. (Pressing with a smaller pie plate or custard cup works well.) Microwave at High 1½ minutes, rotating ½ turn after 1 minute. Cool.

In medium mixing bowl soften cream cheese at High 30 to 45 seconds. Beat in eggs; add sugar, lemon juice and peel. Blend in sour cream.

Reduce power to 50% (Medium). Microwave cheese mixture 4 to 5 minutes, or until thoroughly heated, stirring every other minute. Pour into pie crust. Sprinkle with reserved crumbs. Microwave at 50% (Medium) 9 to 12 minutes, or until almost set. Center will be soft set and will firm up as it chills.

Dates, Figs & Raisins

In some areas, dates and figs are available fresh. Ripe fresh dates are plump and shiny with smooth, golden brown skin. Varieties may be soft, semi-dry or dry. Ripe figs are somewhat soft; over-ripe figs have a sour odor. Shape and color varies with the type of fig.

Dried dates, figs, raisins and currants are usually sold in sealed packages which keep for a few months. Unless they are very fresh, raisins and currants should be plumped, especially when used in short-cooking microwave recipes.

Raisin Pie With Sour Cream Topping

1 microwaved 9-in. pie shell, page 118

Filling:
⅔ cup brown sugar
¼ cup all-purpose flour
   Dash nutmeg
2 cups raisins
1 cup water
⅓ cup orange juice
2 tablespoons lemon juice
1 teaspoon orange peel
1 teaspoon lemon peel

Topping:
½ cup whipped topping
¼ cup sour cream
1 tablespoon brown sugar
¼ cup chopped walnuts

Makes 9-in. pie

In medium mixing bowl or 2-qt. casserole combine filling ingredients. Microwave at High 7 to 8 minutes, or until thickened and bubbly, stirring every 2 minutes. Let cool slightly. Pour into shell. Refrigerate until completely cooled.

In medium bowl combine whipped topping, sour cream and brown sugar. Spread or dollop topping on pie. Sprinkle with nuts.

How to Store Dates, Figs & Raisins

Refrigerate fresh dates and figs in sealed containers. Use figs immediately, as they are highly perishable. Unopened packages of dried fruits may be kept at room temperature. Place contents of opened packages in sealed containers in the crisper to avoid drying and hardening.

How to Plump Raisins

Place 1 cup raisins or currants in dish. Sprinkle with 2 tablespoons water; cover with plastic wrap. Microwave at High 1 to 1½ minutes, stirring once. Let stand 3 to 5 minutes.

Cheesy Date Bars

    5 tablespoons butter or
      margarine
1½ cups finely crushed
      gingersnaps
1½ cups chopped dates
   ⅓ cup water
    1 tablespoon lemon juice
    1 pkg. (8 oz.) cream cheese

Makes 8 × 8-in. dish

Place butter in 8 × 8-in. baking dish. Microwave at High 45 to 60 seconds, or until butter melts. Stir in crumbs until completely coated with butter. Reserve 2 tablespoons crumb mixture. Press remaining crumb mixture firmly and evenly into bottom of dish. Microwave at High 1½ minutes.

In medium bowl combine dates, water and lemon juice. Microwave at High 2½ to 3 minutes, or until thickened, stirring after each minute. Let cool.

Add cream cheese to cooled date mixture. Beat at medium speed until thoroughly blended. Spread over gingersnap crust. Top with reserved crumb mixture. Refrigerate until chilled and set.

No Bake Fruit Cake ▶

    2 cups minced, candied fruits
    1 cup raisins
    1 cup chopped dates
    1 cup chopped nuts
    2 cups graham cracker
      crumbs
    6 tablespoons butter or
      margarine
    1 pkg. (10 oz.) miniature
      marshmallows
   ½ teaspoon rum extract

Makes 9 × 5-in. loaf

Line sides and bottom of 9 × 5-in. loaf dish with foil. In large bowl combine fruits and nuts. Add graham cracker crumbs, tossing to coat. Set fruit mixture aside.

In medium bowl, microwave butter at High 1 to 1½ minutes or until melted. Stir in marshmallows and extract. Microwave at High 1½ to 2 minutes, or until marshmallow mixture is smooth and melted, stirring after 1 minute. Add to fruit mixture.

Stir until ingredients are well distributed and evenly coated. Turn into prepared pan. Press down firmly. Refrigerate until completely chilled. To serve, cut into thin slices.

Raisin Pudding Cake With Hard Sauce ▲

Pudding:

 3 cups soft bread cubes
⅔ cup milk
 2 eggs, slightly beaten
 1 cup all-purpose flour
½ cup butter or margarine,
   melted
¼ cup brown sugar
 2 tablespoons light molasses
 2 teaspoons cinnamon
 1 teaspoon baking soda
¼ teaspoon salt
¼ teaspoon nutmeg

½ cup raisins, plumped, page
   135
 1 cup currants, plumped, page
   135
 1 teaspoon grated lemon peel
 2 tablespoons brandy

Hard Sauce:

½ cup butter or margarine,
   room temperature
1¾ to 2 cups confectioners'
   sugar
1½ to 2 tablespoons brandy
 2 teaspoons water

Serves 6 to 8

Combine bread cubes, milk and eggs in mixing bowl. Stir in remaining pudding ingredients.

Spread batter evenly in 9-in. glass ring mold. Cover with plastic wrap. Place mold on trivet or inverted cereal bowl in oven. Microwave at High 3 minutes, rotating after each minute. Reduce power to 50% (Medium). Microwave 2 to 8 minutes, or until cake springs back, rotating dish ¼ turn every 2 to 3 minutes during cooking. Uncover and let stand directly on countertop 5 minutes. Loosen edges well and turn out onto serving platter.

To make hard sauce, beat butter with mixer 3 minutes, or until light and fluffy. Beat in confectioners' sugar. Add brandy and water. Serve pudding warm, topped with hard sauce.

Raisin & Fig Sauce

 1 tablespoon cornstarch
 1 tablespoon brown sugar
⅛ teaspoon cinnamon
 1 cup apple cider
 2 drops red food coloring
½ cup raisins
½ cup chopped figs

Makes about 2 cups

In 1 to 1½-qt. casserole combine cornstarch, brown sugar and cinnamon. Mix in apple cider. Microwave at High 3 to 4 minutes, or until thickened and bubbly, stirring twice during cooking.

Add food coloring, raisins and figs. Microwave at High 1 minute to heat. Serve with ham or pork.

Grapes

Once grapes are picked, they do not ripen further or improve in sweetness. They are available year-round; the peak season is July through November.

How to Select & Store Grapes

Look for dark varieties with no tinge of green, and white or green grapes with an amber coloring. Fully ripe grapes are fairly soft to the touch, but should be firmly attached to the stems. Store grapes in plastic bags for humidity, refrigerate and use as soon as possible.

Herbed Red Grapes

 2 cups red grapes
¼ cup butter or margarine
¼ teaspoon basil
¼ teaspoon salt
⅛ teaspoon pepper
 1 tablespoon white or rosé
    wine

Serves 4 to 6

Make small cut in grapes; remove seeds. Place butter in small dish. Microwave at High 45 to 60 seconds, or until melted. Stir in basil, salt and pepper. Preheat microwave browning dish at High 3 minutes. Pour in seasoned butter mixture. Tilt dish to coat. Stir in seeded grapes. Microwave at High 1 to 2 minutes, or until thoroughly heated. Sprinkle with wine. Serve over chicken, fish, pork or lamb chops.

Peaches,
Nectarines
& Apricots

◄ Peaches, nectarines and apricots must be harvested when mature because they do not ripen after picking. A rosy blush does not indicate ripeness or flavor. Select these fruits by the ground color between blushed areas. Apricots are in season during June and July. Peaches and nectarines, available June through September, are interchangeable in recipes.

Peaches Flambé

      3 tablespoons sugar
      2 teaspoons cornstarch
      ¼ cup apricot jam
      ¼ cup water
2½ to 3 cups peeled sliced
            peaches, fresh or
            frozen, defrosted, page 115
      1 teaspoon lemon juice
      2 to 4 tablespoons brandy

Serves 6 to 8

In 1½-qt. casserole combine sugar and cornstarch. Stir in jam and water. Microwave at High 2½ to 3 minutes, or until bubbly and slightly thickened, stirring 2 or 3 times during cooking time.

Meanwhile, combine peaches and lemon juice. Add to thickened sauce. Microwave at High 4 to 5 minutes, or until peaches are tender, stirring after half the cooking time.

Place brandy in small dish. Microwave at High 20 seconds to warm. Stir into peaches, or if desired, pour into ladle; ignite and pour over dessert.

Serve over ice cream.

How to Select Peaches, Nectarines & Apricots

Peaches should have a fruity aroma, be creamy or yellow behind their blush, and yield to slight pressure. Avoid greenish or wrinkled peaches and tan spots which indicate rapidly spreading decay.

Nectarines are yellow-orange between blushed areas. Select smooth, unblemished, firm fruit with slight softening along the seam. Avoid hard, dull, shriveled or soft fruit with skin cracks or punctures.

Apricots range from yellow to orange to red in color. They should be slightly soft, but not mushy or bruised. Avoid very firm, greenish fruits.

How to Store Peaches, Nectarines & Apricots

Keep peaches and nectarines at room temperature until soft enough to eat, then store in the crisper in an open container. Use as soon as possible.

Refrigerate apricots in the crisper immediately and use within 2 to 3 days. To prevent light bruising, place fruit in an open container to keep it from rolling when the drawer is opened.

How to Peel Peaches, Nectarines & Apricots

Measure 4 cups water into 2-qt. container. Microwave at High 8 to 11 minutes, or until water boils.

Place 3 peaches, 3 nectarines or 6 to 8 apricots in water. Let fruit stand in water 1 to 1½ minutes to loosen skins.

Remove and immerse in cold water. Skin will peel easily. If necessary, reheat water to boiling and continue with remaining fruit.

Nectarine or Peach Pie ▲

1 microwaved 9-in. pie shell, page 118
4 cups peeled, sliced peaches or nectarines, fresh or frozen, defrosted, page 115, drained
½ tablespoon lemon juice
⅓ cup brown sugar
⅓ cup sugar
¼ cup all-purpose flour
½ teaspoon cinnamon

Topping:
2 tablespoons butter or margarine
¼ cup brown sugar
1½ cups whole wheat flakes cereal, slightly crushed
¼ teaspoon cinnamon

Makes 9-in. pie

Toss peaches with lemon juice. Stir in sugars, flour and cinnamon. Turn into pie shell. Set pie on wax paper in oven. Microwave at High 7 to 13 minutes, or until bubbly in center, rotating ¼ turn every 2 to 4 minutes.

Melt butter in medium bowl or casserole at High 40 to 50 seconds. Mix in brown sugar. Add remaining topping ingredients. Sprinkle evenly over pie. Microwave at High 1 to 1½ minutes to heat.

Fresh Peach Crisp

5 cups peeled, sliced fresh peaches
1 tablespoon lemon juice
½ cup granulated or brown sugar
2 tablespoons all-purpose flour
¼ teaspoon nutmeg

Topping:
¼ cup butter or margarine, melted
⅓ cup brown sugar
½ cup plus 2 tablespoons all-purpose flour
½ cup quick-cooking rolled oats

Serves 8

In medium bowl toss peaches with lemon juice. Add brown sugar, flour and nutmeg. Stir to combine. Pour into 1-qt. casserole. Microwave at High 5 to 7 minutes, or until peaches are tender and sauce is clear and thickened. Set aside.

In small bowl combine topping ingredients. Crumble over peaches. Microwave at High 2 to 4 minutes, or until hot and bubbly. Serve warm or cold, plain or topped with whipped cream or ice cream.

Spiced Apricots

1 tablespoon cornstarch
3 tablespoons sugar
1 cup apricot nectar
⅛ teaspoon cinnamon
⅛ teaspoon ground cloves
8 fresh apricots, peeled, halved and pitted

Serves 4 to 6

In 2-qt. casserole combine cornstarch and sugar. Stir in apricot nectar and spices. Microwave at High 2½ to 4 minutes, or until mixture thickens, stirring every minute.

Stir in apricots. Microwave at High 2 to 4 minutes, or until apricots are fork tender, stirring after half the cooking time. Serve hot or cold.

Peach Conserve

3 cups peeled, pitted, finely chopped peaches
¾ cup dark seedless raisins
½ medium orange, halved and sliced wafer thin
½ medium lemon, halved and sliced wafer thin
¼ teaspoon cinnamon
4½ cups sugar
1 pouch (3 oz.) liquid fruit pectin
½ cup chopped nuts
¼ cup brandy, optional

Makes 6 cups

In 2-qt. measure or 3-qt. casserole combine peaches, raisins, orange and lemon slices, cinnamon and sugar. Microwave at High 12 to 14 minutes, or until mixture comes to a full rolling boil, stirring every 3 minutes. Boil 1 minute.

Stir in pectin, nuts and brandy. Pour into hot sterilized glasses and seal.

Nectarine Upside-Down ▶ Gingerbread Cake

¼ cup butter or margarine
½ cup brown sugar
1 tablespoon milk
2 cups peeled, sliced fresh
  nectarines
1 pkg. (14.5 oz.) gingerbread
  mix

Makes 8 × 8-in. cake

How to Microwave Nectarine Upside-Down Gingerbread Cake

Melt butter in 8 × 8-in. dish at High 1 to 1½ minutes. Blend in sugar and milk. Microwave at High 1½ to 2 minutes, or until slightly thickened and syrupy, stirring once or twice.

Arrange nectarine slices on top. Prepare gingerbread as directed on package. Spoon batter evenly over fruit.

Place dish on inverted saucer. Reduce power to 50% (Medium). Microwave 6 minutes, rotating ¼ turn every 2 minutes. Increase power to High.

Microwave 4 to 8 minutes, or until gingerbread springs back when lightly touched, rotating ¼ turn every 1 or 2 minutes.

Cool directly on countertop 5 minutes. Loosen edges well; turn out onto large platter.

Serve warm. If desired, top with whipped cream or ice cream.

Pears

Pears are picked when mature but still hard; they develop their best flavor when they ripen off the tree. Pears ripen from the inside out, so don't wait until the surface is completely soft, or the center may be brown and mealy. The most common pears are yellow or red Bartletts, D'Anjou, Bosc and Comice.

◄ Lemon Pears & Cream

½ cup water
1 cup sugar
1 small lemon, thinly sliced
6 ripe medium Bartlett pears

Lemon Custard:

¼ cup sugar
½ teaspoon lemon peel
1 tablespoon cornstarch
1 cup half and half
2 egg yolks, slightly beaten
½ teaspoon vanilla

Serves 6

In 2-qt. casserole combine water, sugar and lemon slices. Cover. Microwave at High 3 to 4 minutes, or until mixture boils. Peel pears, leaving stems in. Arrange pears upright in casserole, placing one in center. Baste with sauce. Cover. Microwave at High 7 to 11 minutes, or until pears are fork tender. Cover; refrigerate.

In small bowl or 1-qt. measure combine sugar, peel and cornstarch. Blend in half and half. Microwave at High 1½ to 4 minutes, or until mixture boils and is slightly thickened, stirring every 30 seconds. Blend small amount of thickened mixture into egg yolks. Return egg mixture back to thickened sauce and blend. Reduce power to 50% (Medium). Microwave 1 to 1½ minutes, or until very hot, stirring every 30 seconds. Stir in vanilla. Cover and chill. Serve pears with lemon custard sauce.

How to Select Pears

Look for firm pears which have started to soften at the stem end. Minor surface scars do not affect quality. Pictured left to right: Bartletts are bell-shaped with thin skin which is red or yellow and may be blushed. Comice pears are round with thick, yellow-green skin and some russeting. Bosc pears have a long neck and dark yellow skin with cinnamon-colored russeting. Color is no indication of ripeness with D'Anjou pears, which range from yellow to green.

How to Store Pears

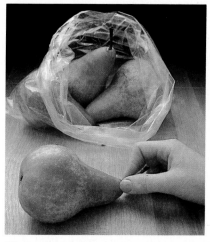

Ripen hard pears at room temperature until skin at stem end yields to gentle pressure. If kept in plastic bag, open or perforate it. Refrigerate ripened pears uncovered in the crisper; use as soon as possible.

Pear Preserves

4 cups peeled, cored, finely
    chopped Bartlett pears
1 tablespoon lemon juice
3 cups sugar
⅛ teaspoon ground cloves,
    optional
1 teaspoon grated lemon peel
1 pouch (3 oz.) liquid fruit
    pectin

Makes 4½ cups

Combine pears, lemon juice, sugar, cloves and lemon peel in 3-qt. casserole or 2-qt. measure. Microwave at High 10 to 15 minutes, or until mixture comes to a full rolling boil, stirring 2 or 3 times during cooking. Boil 1 minute.

Mix in pectin thoroughly. Skim off foam. Store in refrigerator or pour into hot sterilized jars, seal and process.

Pear Mincemeat Pie ▶

1 microwaved 9-in. pie shell
    with cut outs, page 118
1 pkg. (9 oz.) condensed
    mincemeat
1 cup water
3 ripe medium pears, peeled,
    cored and chopped

Makes 9-in. pie

Crumble mincemeat into 1-qt. measure or small mixing bowl. Add water. Microwave at High 6 minutes, or until mixture is cooked, stirring after half the cooking time. Mix in pears.

Turn mincemeat mixture into prepared shell. Set pie on wax paper in oven. Microwave at High 9 to 15 minutes, or until pears are tender and filling appears hot and bubbly in center, rotating ¼ turn every 3 minutes. Prepare lattice top as directed on page 118.

Pineapple

Contrary to popular belief, pineapples should be harvested when ripe, as they do not ripen further after picking. If they are held at room temperature, the shell may change color and soften, but this does not improve flavor. Pulling the leaves or thumping the fruit are not tests of quality. Size, weight and freshness are. Pineapple is available all year, but the peak season is March to June.

How to Select & Store Pineapple

Choose large pineapples which are heavy for their size; they yield a greater proportion of edible fruit. Fresh-looking, dark green crown leaves and sweet fragrance are signs of quality. Slight separation between the eyes indicates maturity. Avoid fruit with bruises, soft spots and dry or brown leaves.

Refrigerate pineapple in the crisper, and use as soon as possible. A change in shell color or softening results from holding too long rather than from ripening.

How to Prepare Pineapple

Cut off crown and stem end. Stand pineapple upright and slice off rind in narrow, lengthwise strips, leaving as much fruit as possible.

Remove eyes by making shallow diagonal cut on both sides of each row of eyes. Quarter pineapple and remove core. Slice fruit in chunks, fingers or wedges.

Make "boats" by cutting pineapple lengthwise through crown in wedges. Remove core; loosen fruit with sharp grapefruit knife, leaving ½-in. shell. Slice.

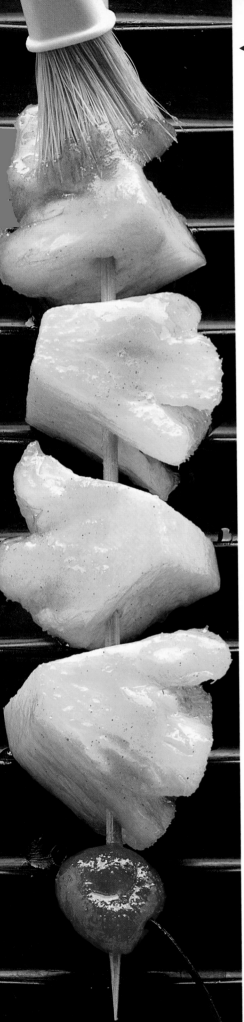

◀ Pineapple Kabobs

8 wooden skewers,
   10 in. long
32 fresh pineapple chunks, 1-in.
2 tablespoons butter or
   margarine

1 tablespoon light rum or
   water
⅓ cup brown sugar
¼ teaspoon cinnamon
8 maraschino cherries

Serves 8

On each skewer place 4 pineapple chunks. Arrange on rack in 12 × 8-in. baking dish. Set aside.

In small dish microwave butter at High 30 to 60 seconds or until melted. Stir in rum. Add brown sugar and cinnamon.

Brush one-third of mixture on pineapple chunks. Cover with wax paper. Microwave at High 2 minutes. Turn over and rearrange skewers. Brush with one-third of sugar mixture. Re-cover. Microwave at High 2 to 3 minutes, or until hot.

Brush with remaining brown sugar mixture. Top each skewer with a cherry. Re-cover. Let stand 1 to 2 minutes, or until sugar melts.

Pineapple Chutney ▼

2 cans (20 oz. each) crushed
   pineapple, drained and
   ½ cup juice reserved
1½ cups raisins
¾ cup cider vinegar
⅔ cup brown sugar
⅓ cup chopped green pepper
¼ cup chopped onion

2 cloves garlic, pressed or
   minced
2 tablespoons finely chopped
   crystallized ginger
½ teaspoon salt
¼ teaspoon cinnamon
⅛ teaspoon ground cloves
⅛ teaspoon cayenne pepper

Makes about 6 cups

Place pineapple and reserved liquid in 3-qt. casserole; mash. Combine with remaining ingredients; cover. Microwave at High 10 minutes, stirring after half the cooking time.

Remove cover. Microwave at High 15 to 20 minutes, or until of desired consistency, stirring every 5 minutes.

Mixture can be stored in refrigerator or ladled into hot sterilized jars, sealed and processed. Serve as a relish with all meats.

Pineapple Upside-Down Cake ▲

1/4 cup butter or margarine
1/4 cup brown sugar
2 tablespoons honey
1 can (8 oz.) pineapple rings,
   1/3 cup juice reserved

9 maraschino cherries, well
   drained, optional
Pecan halves, optional
1 pkg. (9 oz.) yellow cake mix
   (one layer size)
1 egg

Serves 8

Place butter in 8 × 8-in. baking dish or 9-in. round cake dish. Microwave at High 45 to 60 seconds, or until melted. Spread evenly over bottom of dish. Sprinkle with sugar; drizzle with honey.

Top with pineapple rings, cutting to fit as necessary. Place cherries in centers of rings. Arrange pecan halves around rings. Place dish on inverted saucer. Microwave at High 3 minutes.

Blend cake mix, reserved juice and egg in medium mixing bowl on low speed of electric mixer. Beat at medium speed 2 minutes. Spoon batter evenly over fruit.

Place dish on inverted saucer. Reduce power to 50% (Medium). Microwave 5 minutes, rotating 1/4 turn twice during cooking time. Increase power to High. Microwave 2 to 5 minutes, or until toothpick inserted in center comes out clean.

Cool directly on countertop 5 minutes. Loosen edges well and turn out onto plate. Serve warm with whipped cream.

Sundae Topping

1/4 cup sugar
1 1/2 tablespoons cornstarch
1 can (13 1/4 oz.) crushed
   pineapple in unsweetened
   juice
1/4 cup water
1 teaspoon lemon peel
2 tablespoons honey

Makes about 2 cups

In 1 to 1 1/2-qt. casserole combine sugar and cornstarch. Add remaining ingredients.

Microwave at High 5 to 6 minutes, or until thickened, stirring every other minute. Chill. Serve over ice cream.

Plums & Prunes

Plums are available June through September. The many varieties of plums differ significantly in shape, color, flavor and texture. Some are very juicy, others more mealy. Italian prune plums, a variety of plums, are dried to produce prunes. Fresh prune plums have purple-black or blue-black skin which turns deep red when cooked. The pit of fresh prune plums separates easily from the flesh, which is less juicy and tart than most plums.

◄ Sugared Plums

¼ cup butter or margarine
½ cup sugar
1 teaspoon cinnamon
6 large ripe plums, halved
   and pitted

Serves 4 to 6

In small dish, melt butter at High 50 to 60 seconds. Combine sugar and cinnamon in bowl or on wax paper.

Dip plum halves in butter. Roll in cinnamon-sugar, coating generously. Place in 8 × 8-in. dish or on serving plate. Cover with wax paper. Microwave at High 2 to 3 minutes, or until fork tender, rotating dish and rearranging halves from center to outer edge after half the cooking time. Do not over-cook or plums will lose their shape.

Let stand 1 to 2 minutes. If desired, sprinkle with any remaining cinnamon-sugar before serving with meat or as a meat garnish.

How to Select & Store Plums & Prunes

Look for fruit that is beginning to soften. Color is not an accurate guide as it ranges from yellow-green to red to red-purple. Hard fruit is immature and may shrivel but will not ripen at home. Do not buy fruit which is very soft or shows skin breaks, brownish discolorations or leaking.

Leave firm fruit at room temperature to soften and become juicy; this may take 3 to 4 days. When ripe, store uncovered in the crisper and use promptly.

Plum Cake

3 tablespoons butter or
  margarine
½ cup brown sugar
½ cup chopped nuts
4 small ripe plums, pitted and
  diced (about 1 cup)

Cake:
1 cup all-purpose flour

⅔ cup sugar
1 teaspoon baking powder
½ teaspoon salt
½ teaspoon vanilla
⅓ cup shortening
2 eggs
⅓ cup milk

Makes 9-in. round cake

Line bottom of 9-in. round baking dish with wax paper. Place butter in dish. Microwave at High 45 to 60 seconds, or until melted. Spread butter evenly over bottom of dish. Sprinkle with sugar and nuts. Microwave at High 2 minutes, rotating ½ turn after 1 minute. Top with diced plums. Set aside.

Place all cake ingredients in mixing bowl. Blend at low speed, then beat at medium speed 2 minutes.

Spoon cake batter evenly over fruit. Place dish on inverted saucer in oven. Reduce power to 50% (Medium). Microwave 6 minutes, rotating ¼ turn every 1 to 2 minutes. Increase power to High.

Microwave 3 to 7½ minutes, or until top springs back and appears baked. Cool directly on countertop 5 minutes. Loosen edges well and turn out onto plate. Serve warm, plain or with whipped cream.

Braised Plums

¼ cup water
2 teaspoons cornstarch
½ cup honey

10 Italian prune plums
  or 6 medium ripe plums

Serves 4

Combine water and cornstarch in 1½ to 2-qt. casserole. Stir in honey. Microwave at High 2½ to 3 minutes, or until thickened and bubbly, stirring 2 or 3 times during cooking.

Prick each plum twice with fork to prevent bursting. Add to honey sauce, turning to coat. Cover. Microwave at High 3 to 6 minutes, or until plums are fork tender, stirring each minute during cooking. Let stand 3 minutes.

Prune Oatmeal Muffins

1 cup flour (½ whole wheat,
  if desired)
½ cup quick-cooking rolled oats
½ cup brown sugar
1½ teaspoons baking powder
½ teaspoon salt
½ cup milk
⅓ cup vegetable oil or
  melted shortening
1 egg
½ cup chopped and pitted
  dried prunes*
½ teaspoon grated lemon peel
½ cup chopped nuts, optional

Makes 12 muffins

Line custard cups or microwave cupcake dish with two paper liners. Place all ingredients except nuts in mixing bowl. Mix only until particles are moistened. Fill cups half full. Sprinkle with nuts, if desired.

Arrange custard cups in ring when microwaving 3 or more. Microwave at High as directed in chart. Rotate and rearrange after half the cooking time. Remove muffins from cups to wire rack after baking.

*Chopped dates or chopped figs can be substituted.

1 muffin	½ to ¾ min.
2 muffins	1 min.
4 muffins	1½ to 2 min.
6 muffins	2¼ to 3 min.

Rhubarb

Tart, refreshing rhubarb is available in spring and early summer, especially March through May. Rhubarb can be red, pink or green, depending on the variety, soil and growing conditions. If you grow your own rhubarb, pull, rather than cut, young stems to encourage new growth. Remove and dispose of leaves, which contain oxalic acid and can be poisonous.

How to Select & Store Rhubarb

Choose firm, crisp, brightly colored stalks. Young stems with immature leaves will be most tender and delicate in flavor.

Avoid very thin or overly large and tough stalks. Discard leaves.

Wrap loosely in plastic wrap. Refrigerated, fresh stalks keep well up to 4 weeks, but wilt rapidly at room temperature.

How to Microwave Rhubarb Sauce

Cut rhubarb into 1-in. pieces. In 1½ to 2-qt. casserole, combine 2 cups rhubarb with ¼ cup water. Cover

Microwave at High 5 to 9½ minutes, or until rhubarb is slightly transparent and tender, stirring after half the time.

Stir in ½ cup sugar and ¼ teaspoon lemon juice. Let stand, covered, 2 to 3 minutes. Stir before serving, adding a few drops red food coloring, if desired.

Rhubarb Cake ►

Cake:

  2 cups all-purpose flour
1½ cups brown sugar
  1 teaspoon baking soda
  1 teaspoon salt
  ½ teaspoon baking powder
  ⅔ cup shortening
  4 eggs
  ⅓ cup milk combined with ½
     tablespoon lemon juice
1½ cups 1-in. rhubarb pieces

Topping:

  ¼ cup sugar
  ¼ cup brown sugar
  ¼ cup chopped nuts
  ½ teaspoon cinnamon

    Whipped cream, optional

      Makes two 9-in. layers

Place all cake ingredients except rhubarb in mixing bowl. Blend at low speed, then beat at medium speed 2 minutes. Stir in rhubarb.

Line bottoms of two 9-in. round layer cake dishes with wax paper. Pour half of cake batter into each dish.

Combine topping ingredients in small bowl. Set aside.

Microwave 1 layer at a time at 50% (Medium) 6 minutes, rotating ¼ turn after 3 minutes. Increase power to High. Microwave 3 minutes. Sprinkle with half the topping mixture. Microwave 1 to 1½ minutes longer, or until toothpick inserted in center comes out clean. Let stand directly on countertop 5 to 10 minutes. (Repeat for second layer.)

If desired, spread whipped cream between layers.

Rhubarb & Custard Pie

  1 microwaved 9-in. pie shell,
    page 118
  3 cups rhubarb pieces, fresh
    or frozen, defrosted, page
    115, drained
  ¾ cup sugar
  2 tablespoons all-purpose flour
  ¼ teaspoon salt
  2 eggs
  ½ cup cream
  2 tablespoons sugar
  ¼ teaspoon nutmeg

      Makes 9-in. pie

In medium bowl combine rhubarb, sugar, flour and salt. Place in prepared pie shell.

Microwave at High 6 minutes, rotating ½ turn after 3 minutes. Carefully spoon thickened filling from edge to center. Let cool 5 minutes. Meanwhile, beat together eggs, cream, sugar and nutmeg. Reduce power to 50% (Medium). Microwave 1 to 2 minutes, or until lukewarm, stirring after 1 minute. Carefully pour over rhubarb.

Microwave at 50% (Medium) 6 to 12 minutes, or until custard is set, rotating ¼ turn every 2 minutes. Let cool.

Strawberry Rhubarb Sauce

  2 cups 1-in. rhubarb pieces
  2 tablespoons water
  1 tablespoon cornstarch
  1 pkg. (10 oz.) frozen,
    sweetened strawberries,
    defrosted, page 115,
    drained, juice reserved
  ⅓ to ½ cup sugar

      Makes 2 cups

In 1½ to 2-qt. casserole combine rhubarb and water. Cover. Microwave at High 3 to 4 minutes, or until rhubarb is tender, but still in whole pieces.

In small bowl combine cornstarch and strawberry juice. Add to rhubarb with strawberries. Microwave, uncovered, 3 to 5 minutes, or until clear and thickened, stirring after half the cooking time.

Stir in sugar. Cover; let stand 2 to 3 minutes before serving.

Fruit Combinations

Contrast is the secret of appealing fruit combinations. Mix delicate and bright colors, crisp and smooth textures, bland and distinctive or tart and sweet flavors. Use some fresh fruits in season with frozen and canned fruits.

◄ Fruit Soup

1 pkg. (8 oz.) dried mixed fruit
1 cup dried apricots
½ cup raisins
5½ cups water, divided
3 cinnamon sticks
¼ to ½ cup quick-cooking tapioca
1 medium orange, thinly sliced
¾ cup sugar
⅓ cup currant jelly

Serves 6 to 8

In 3-qt. casserole combine mixed fruit, apricots, raisins, 3 cups water and cinnamon sticks. Cover. Microwave at High 10 minutes, stirring once during cooking.

Stir in tapioca. Cover. Microwave at High 5 minutes longer, or until fruit is tender.

Add 2½ cups water and remaining ingredients. Re-cover; microwave at High 2 to 4 minutes, or until flavors are blended and tapioca is tender, stirring once. Let stand 2 to 3 minutes. Remove cinnamon sticks. Serve warm or cool.

Variation:
Substitute ½ cup brandy for ½ cup of water.

Baked Ambrosia ▶

2 large oranges
1 can (8 oz.) pineapple
    chunks, drained
1½ tablespoons brown sugar
1 tablespoon honey
2 tablespoons coconut
4 maraschino cherries

Serves 4

Cut oranges in half crosswise. Free fruit from shell carefully with a grapefruit knife. Separate orange sections.

Toss together orange sections, pineapple, brown sugar, honey and coconut in mixing bowl. Mound into shells. Top each with a cherry. Place shells on serving platter or individual serving dishes.

Microwave at High 2½ to 3 minutes, or until heated through, rotating and rearranging after half the cooking time.

Variation:
Substitute ½ cup fresh seedless green grapes for pineapple.

Ruby Fruit Combo

1 pkg. (10 oz.) frozen
    sweetened raspberries,
    defrosted, page 115, drained
    and juice reserved
3 tablespoons sugar
2 tablespoons cornstarch
1 cup frozen, pitted dark sweet
    cherries, defrosted, page 115
2 cups thickly sliced fresh
    strawberries
1 teaspoon lemon juice

Makes 1 qt.

In 1½ to 2-qt. casserole combine raspberry juice, sugar and cornstarch. Microwave at High 2½ to 3 minutes, or until thick and bubbly, stirring once or twice during cooking.

Stir in fruit and lemon juice. Serve with whipped cream or over cake.

Pudding Glaze for Mixed Fruit Salad

1 pkg. (3 to 3⅝ oz.) vanilla
    pudding mix
½ cup milk
1 cup orange juice
¼ cup water
7 to 8 cups fruit, fresh
    or canned, drained
1 cup miniature
    marshmallows

Serves 6 to 8

In 1 to 1½-qt. casserole or medium mixing bowl combine pudding and milk. Stir in juice and water.

Microwave at High 4 to 5 minutes, or until mixture boils and is slightly thickened, stirring after 3 minutes and then every minute. Refrigerate until cold.

Stir in fruit and 1 cup marshmallows. Chill several hours.

NOTE: Use a combination of such fruits as pears, peaches, apples, oranges, etc. Juice drained from any canned fruits may be used in the salad.

Peach Raspberry Sauce

1 pkg. (10 oz.) frozen
    sweetened raspberries,
    defrosted, page 115,
    drained, juice reserved
1 tablespoon cornstarch
1 cup peeled sliced fresh
    peaches
1½ to 2 tablespoons sweet
    wine or liqueur

Makes about 1½ cups.

In 1 to 1½-qt. casserole combine raspberry juice and cornstarch. Stir in raspberries. Microwave at High 2½ to 4 minutes, or until thickened and bubbly, stirring after 2 minutes and then every minute.

Add peaches and wine. Microwave at High 30 seconds.

Serve over ice cream.

Variation:
Substitute 1 can (16 oz.) sliced peaches, drained for the fresh.

Index